WAGNER E. 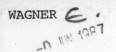 | Swords and daggers. | 6274221

-0 MAY 1987

739.72

HERTFORDSHIRE LIBRARY SERVICE

D1454677

Please renew/return this item by the last date shown.

So that your telephone call is charged at local rate, please call the numbers as set out below:

	From Area codes 01923 or 0208:	From the rest of Herts:
Renewals:	01923 471373	01438 737373
Enquiries:	01923 471333	01438 737333
Minicom:	01923 471599	01438 737599

L32b

SWORDS AND DAGGERS

Figura per il Cap. XIX

Figura per il Cap. XX.

Swords and Daggers

Text and illustrations by
Eduard Wagner

Hamlyn
London · New York · Sydney · Toronto

Translated by Jean Layton
Graphic design by Aleš Krejča
Designed and produced by Artia for
The Hamlyn Publishing Group Limited
London · New York · Sydney ·Toronto
Astronaut House, Feltham, Middlesex, England

Copyright © Artia 1975

ISBN 0 600 38100 5

Printed in Czechoslovakia by Polygrafia

CONTENTS

INTRODUCTION

Swords and daggers belong to the category of weapons which, in hand-to-hand fighting, depend exclusively on the strength and speed of the arm.

These weapons may be identified by their long and fairly narrow blades, the shape of which was determined by the fighting habits of a tribe, a nation, a state or simply by the area of origin and date of development. The *blade* was sharpened on one or both edges and was either smooth or channelled in various ways with grooves intended to lighten the blade, and the tip was usually pointed. The far shorter *grip,* by which the weapon was grasped and wielded, was secured either by the *pommel* or the *back-strap.* The hand was protected either by *quillons* placed between the blade and the grip, or later by a series of *bars,* or a complete *basket,* enclosing the whole hand. (One exception was the Russian Cossack sabre, which had no guard at all for the hand). The blade was joined to the hilt by means of the *tang* running through the whole hilt. These weapons are classified by the style, blade, hilt and method of use.

CUT AND THRUST WEAPONS WITH BLADES

a) straight

b) curved

swords

sabres

rapiers

broadswords

AUSTRIAN CAVALRY SABRE, MODEL 1904

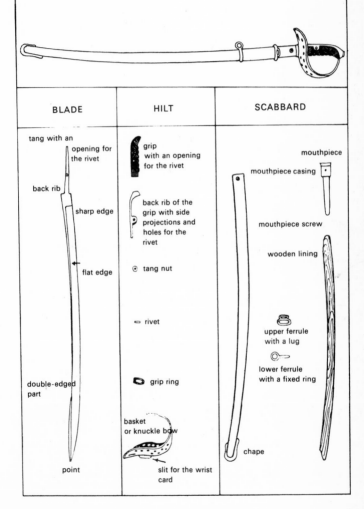

BLADE	HILT	SCABBARD
tang with an opening for the rivet	grip with an opening for the rivet	mouthpiece
back rib	back rib of the grip with side projections and holes for the rivet	mouthpiece casing
sharp edge	tang nut	mouthpiece screw
flat edge	rivet	wooden lining
double-edged part	grip ring	upper ferrule with a lug
		lower ferrule with a fixed ring
	basket or knuckle bow	
point	slit for the wrist card	chape

THE SWORD

The first type of cut and thrust weapon was the sword which survived for the longest period on the European battlefields and whose history is embellished with numerous legends.

This weapon has a broad straight blade sharpened on both edges with a point that is in line with the centre of the blade. Although used both by the Greek and Roman heavily armoured infantry, the sword achieved its greatest importance following the overthrow of the Roman Empire. The leading role played by the disciplined infantry phalanx in the field of battle was usurped by the somewhat undisciplined, boastfully proud and courageous knight on horseback who was more interested in his own honour than in the efficiency of the army as a whole. It was he who brought the sword as his main weapon to the battlefield. The sword was adapted to combat on horseback and this resulted in the lengthening of the blade. The equestrian knight was also equipped with protective armour such as the helmet, cuirass and shield. The lance was still used for the first attack of the battle. The later development of the missile weapon such as the crossbow and firearm meant that the knights needed stronger protective armour, which in turn evoked certain changes in the design of the cutting weapons. In close combat the cut was now less effective and the blade underwent certain changes to allow the swordsman to thrust at vulnerable joints where the plates of armour met. The blade was made rigid, heavier and stronger. The cut was of course still used, but it was now often necessary to wield the sword with both hands and the grip therefore had to be lengthened. Such changes do not prove that the thrust was not used in earlier times but only that the fighter now had to seek out the weak points in his opponent's armour. This method of fighting demanded not only strength but also agility and swift thinking.

The pommel of the sword, which held the grip fast to the tang and acted as a counterweight, also took on a different appearance; it became more massive—not only to balance the sword but also to enable the knight to use it for direct blows when he could not stretch his arm for a cut with the blade. Talhoffer's illustrated *Fechtbuch,* a handbook on combat dating from 1467 (published by Gustav Hergsell in Prague, 1887) depicts various blows delivered with the pommel of a sword being held by the blade.

The cross-guard or quillons were lengthened in order to prevent the hand from slipping on to the blade when thrusting, and to protect the hand from the blade of the opponent's weapon, which, when countering a cut, might slide right up the attacker's blade. As early as the twelfth, and above all in the thirteenth century, we come across quillons that droop slightly at both ends, with the aim of catching the opponent's blade better.

To control the blade better with one hand, the swordsman would hook his forefinger over the quillons towards the blade to prevent it from turning from the direction of the cut. This method of holding the weapon led to certain structural changes aimed at protecting the forefinger which was endangered in spite of the gauntlet protecting it. By the end of the fifteenth century we come across a bar jutting out and back round towards the blade from the root of the quillons to protect the forefinger. At the point where it was held by the forefinger the blade was blunted and became known as the *ricasso*. This change formed the basis for the future development both in the protection of the hand and in the shape of the blade.

The above-mentioned bars, known as the arms of the hilt, were later combined with side rings developed to protect the hand at the centre of the cross-guard, independently of the arms. Later on appeared other guards at the end of the arms of the hilt which were linked by means of connecting bars or counterguards with the side rings on the quillons.

The grip, often spirally ribbed and wound with plaited wire, again became shorter, for use with one hand only.

Between the sharp edge of the blade and the cross-guard there remained a smooth-edged section, the ricasso, protected by the various bars.

THE PARTS OF A SWORD

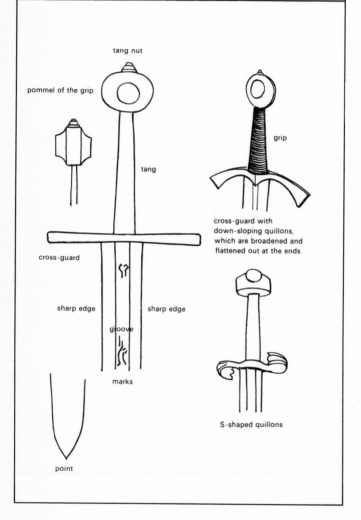

tang nut

pommel of the grip

tang

grip

cross-guard

cross-guard with down-sloping quillons, which are broadened and flattened out at the ends

sharp edge

sharp edge

groove

marks

S-shaped quillons

point

These changes in the hilt are characteristic of the Renaissance sword, whose quillons acquired more counter-guards linking it with the front knuckle bow. This was formed by a rib rising from the front arm of the quillons and curving up towards the pommel of the sword. This was how the originally simple cross-guard developed into the complex basket for the protection of the hand and gradually took the place of the gauntlet. From the middle of the seventeenth century the shapes of the basket generally became simpler. One reason for this was, no doubt, the Thirty Years' War which demanded that the manufacturers and blade-makers' workshops produce in the shortest possible time a larger number of identical weapons for the battlefield.

THE TWO-HANDED SWORD

In the second half of the fifteenth century the two-handed sword, about 150 cm long, began to come into common use for infantry fighting. The manner in which this sword was used is depicted in the *Fechtbuch* by Talhoffer.

The most widespread use of the two-handed sword occurred during the first half of the sixteenth century when the mercenary Landsknecht had regiments in which specially trained experts were equipped with these swords. The whole sword was as tall, indeed sometimes even taller, than a man. Its blade always had a straight longitudinal axis, but its edge could be straight or wavy, or at times even filed down into semi-circular scallops. The grip was long, covered with leather and ending in a large pommel. Between the grip and the blade itself there was a longish ricasso, from each side of which there would protrude a pointed spike, usually drooping slightly towards the point. To enable the soldiers to catch hold of the blade with safety, the ricasso was frequently covered with leather. With sufficient training the two-handed sword could even be used for fencing. It weighed from 4 to 5.25 kg. The cross-guard was usually long, with downward sloping arms, often spirally twisted and ornamented, and there were two large ring guards on either side of the centre of the quillons.

THE EXECUTIONER'S SWORD

The executioner's sword does not really fit into the scope of this book, for in the true sense of the word it is not a weapon but an instrument. The blade was usually about 80 cm long and 5 cm broad, with straight parallel edges and no point, indeed its end was rounded and sometimes pierced with three circular holes—perhaps so that it could not be sharpened to a point. The grip was long enough for it to be grasped with both hands and the quillons were very simple. The symbols of the administration of Justice, i.e. the gallows and the executioner's wheel fixed to the stake, were often engraved upon the blade. Various inscriptions were also frequently found on these swords, often pertaining to the condemned man's last affairs.

A block was not used in executions by sword, as opposed to execution by axe. Instead, the condemned man had to kneel with his head slightly bowed and his hands, sometimes holding a cross, bound in front of him. His eyes were frequently covered. The executioner's sword is sometimes, especially in works of art, mistaken for the honourable, two-handed Landsknecht battle-sword.

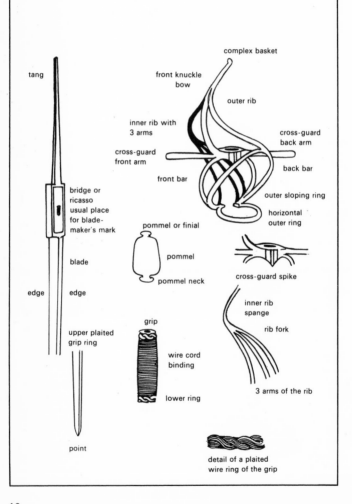

THE PARTS OF A RENAISSANCE RAPIER

tang

complex basket

front knuckle bow

outer rib

inner rib with 3 arms

cross-guard back arm

cross-guard front arm

back bar

front bar

bridge or ricasso usual place for blade-maker's mark

outer sloping ring

horizontal outer ring

pommel or finial

pommel

blade

pommel neck

cross-guard spike

edge

edge

inner rib spange

rib fork

upper plaited grip ring

grip

wire cord binding

lower ring

3 arms of the rib

point

detail of a plaited wire ring of the grip

THE RAPIER

The term rapier is normally used for a weapon with a long, narrow blade, the cross-section of which was often in the form of a flattened hexagon or diamond. Some were scalloped in the same way as the two-handed swords.

The rapier is more of a thrust than a cutting weapon.

The grip was long enough for it to be grasped with one hand, with the forefinger round the quillon and the thumb pressed against the ricasso. The hand was guarded by an elaborately-shaped basket with a knuckle guard, counter-guards and ring guards. The rapier was used in this form from the sixteenth century to the middle of the seventeenth century. The hilts of rapiers carried by noblemen were often remarkable works of art and the ornamentation of the quillons and the pommel was usually uniform in style.

In Italy and Spain during the seventeenth century rapiers were made with deep bell-shaped baskets, richly ornamented with a turned-over rim on the outer side, which was useful for catching the point of the opponent's blade, and a long straight quillon, from which, in most cases, a knuckle bow curved up towards the pommel.

In the second half of the seventeenth century the hilt once again began to assume a simpler form. It consisted of a closed shell supported by a bridge, with either two arms and a knuckle bow or a knuckle bow and a back arm of the quillons; the grip was held fast by the pommel, thus holding the whole hilt together. The rapiers worn by cavaliers at court were particularly richly and delicately ornamented.

THE PARTS OF A BAROQUE RAPIER

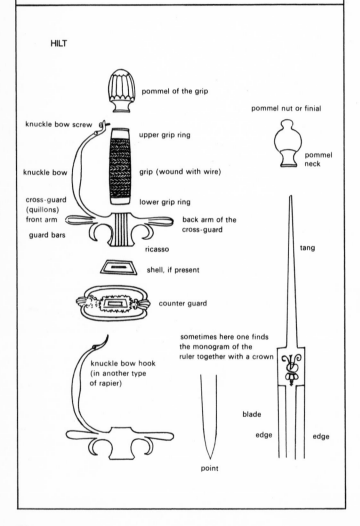

HILT

pommel of the grip

pommel nut or finial

knuckle bow screw

upper grip ring

pommel neck

knuckle bow

grip (wound with wire)

cross-guard
(quillons)
front arm

lower grip ring

back arm of the
cross-guard

guard bars

ricasso

tang

shell, if present

counter guard

sometimes here one finds
the monogram of the
ruler together with a crown

knuckle bow hook
(in another type
of rapier)

blade

edge

edge

point

THE ESTOC

The estoc is a weapon that developed from the thrusting sword and in time acquired such a form that it could be used only for thrusting. It took on its own individual form in the sixteenth, and more in the seventeenth and eighteenth centuries. It was found among the hussars of Polish and Austrian armies which were continually at war with the Turks or the Tatars, who mostly wore armour-plate for protection or clothing of chain-mail—this latter being useful when fighting in hot weather. Thus the climatic conditions resulted in the appearance of a special type of protective clothing, which in turn brought about the development of an effective weapon—the estoc. It had an exceptionally sharp and hard point that could rip open the chains of the coat of mail. The blade was usually between 100 and 150 cm long, sometimes with a triangular or quadrangular cross-section. In some cases the wide blade ended in a long narrow point.

The Polish hussars were equipped with these weapons in the seventeenth century and kept them hanging under the wings of their saddles, parallel to the horse. The hussar riding on horseback had the estoc under his left thigh. At the beginning of the eighteenth century some specialists in the Austrian hussar regiments were also equipped with the estoc. The Austrians carried the weapon in the same way as the Polish hussars, but on the opposite side of the horse. The Polish hussars belonged to the heavy cavalry, whereas the Austrian hussars were a light cavalry.

THE BROADSWORD

In function, the broadsword was a development of the sword and was exclusively a cavalry weapon. It had a straight blade, originally two-edged, later with only one sharp edge. These weapons were uniform in character, especially in the shape of the basket and also in the metal mounts of the scabbard, but preference was given to blades of older origin from workshops of well known blade-makers. In time, however, even these gave way to blades of uniform shape and ornamentation, at first for an individual regiment and later on in whole armies. This process of development was different in each state but (roughly) one can say that this stage of unification was reached by the middle of the eighteenth century.

THE SABRE

The sabre's characteristic feature is its curved blade which allows for the sharp edge to be followed through after the cut itself, thus enlarging the wound.

The sabre can be found depicted in European illuminated manuscripts dating as far back as the fifteenth century. In Central Europe weapons with slightly curved blades and long grips were used towards the end of the fifteenth century and during the sixteenth century. At first they were used by burghers and later on even by some of the nobles, but the sword and the rapier remained the typical weapon of these regions.

On the border of Austria and Hungary during the sixteenth and seventeenth centuries the local people used a sabre which was a combination of a Hungarian blade and a German basket; it was known as the *Bauernwehr* (peasant sword).

The hussars introduced the Hungarian type of sabre into the Western armies, bringing with them also their typical uniform, derived from the Hungarian national costume.

Austria maintained a rule for the equipment of its cavalry according to which the heavy cavalry had simple broadswords, whereas the hussars, and later also the Uhlans, carried sabres. In the middle of the eighteenth century a sabre of unified form was introduced for all types of cavalry.

In the Austrian army the sabre was worn also by the officers of the border guard infantry regiments and also by the officers of the Hungarian infantry.

The appearance of the bayonet in the latter part of the seventeenth century resulted in an important change in the equipment of the infantry. Each infantryman had now become both

THE PARTS OF A SABRE WITH A SLENDER HAND-GUARD

a) grip
b) grip guard
c) pommel finial
d) spike of grip guard
e) knuckle bow
f) cross-guard catches
g) thumb ring
h) hole for the grip-guard spike
i) back arm of the cross-guard
j) cross-guard

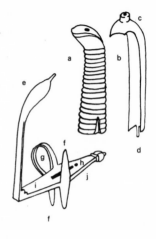

a) grip ring
b) convex knuckle bow
c) semi-circular cross-guard catches
(broad)

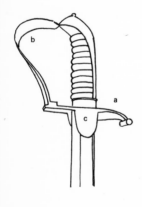

*)
The aim of the cross-guard catches
was to hold the weapon in the
scabbard, which was usually made of
wood. Later a spring was fixed to
the mouth of the scabbard.

a musketeer and a pikeman, considerably increasing his fighting potential. By the beginning of the eighteenth century the long sword that had been part of the equipment of the infantry began to be replaced by a shorter sabre with a slightly curved blade. The infantryman had a better chance of using this shorter weapon even in the thickest turmoil. Many countries discontinued the issue of swords to the infantry during the eighteenth century.

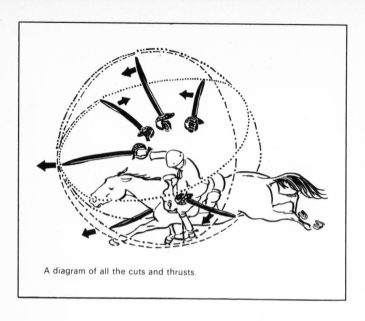

A diagram of all the cuts and thrusts.

THE FALCHION

Into this rather broad grouping we put all the cutting weapons that are shorter than the sword or sabre, but which still have a heavy, either straight or curved, fairly broad blade, or one that broadens towards the point. This weapon usually has only one sharp edge. In some types of the falchion the back of the blade is sharpened with teeth like a saw. In more recent times sapper units were usually equipped with short heavy-bladed weapons, known as sidearms, usually intended to serve also as a cutting tool.

THE YATAGHAN AND THE KINDJHAL

Both these types of weapon originated from the Near East, and were therefore regional weapons, but were nevertheless used in some of the irregular units of the European armies.

The yataghan was in common use in the Balkans; in the Austrian army it was used by the Serbian volunteer regiments. The yataghan had a wavy curved blade with a sharp edge on its concave side. The hilt was split into two wings at the top and had no protection for the fist.

The kindjhal was the typical weapon of the Caucasian mountain fighters. It had a straight blade with two edges and an exceptionally pointed tip. This type of weapon was taken over by the Russian Tsarist army, although in slightly different form. The artillery, the train, and the service corps units were equipped with them.

THE DAGGER

The dagger is a weapon with a short blade, designed for thrusting, and used for close hand-to-hand fighting. The dagger is to be found on the waists of kings, princes and knights, but also beneath the cloaks of assassins. It is this fact that gives the dagger its bad name, making one associate this weapon with assassinations in general. To be sure, weapons with short blades were used for the assassination, in 1306, of the young Czech king Wenceslas III, the last of the Přemyslids, or for the murder of Henry IV of France in 1610, for instance.

The dagger was of course used also in open fighting in situations where the knight was unable to take a swing with the sword. Medieval illuminations depicting the clash of knights in the so-called *mêlée* show how one of the combatants would wind his arm round his opponent's throat, pulling him towards his horse's neck and at the same time stabbing him with a dagger. The manner in which the dagger was used by the swordsman in duels is depicted for instance by Talhoffer in his fencing instruction book of 1476 (the *Fechtbuch*). Talhoffer shows the victor bending down over his rival, removing the armour on his throat and giving the *coup de grâce*, just as he might finish off a hunted animal. Presumably that is where the term used for the dagger, the 'misericord' (derived from the Latin *misericordia*) comes from—by putting him to death by a 'mercy' blow, the victor spared the wounded man from further pain and uncertain fate in the hand of the healer.

The sword and dagger were used separately. The method of combat in which the rapier was held in one hand, usually the right one, and dagger in the other became common only during

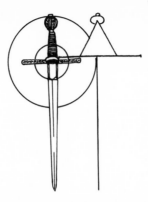

A buckler in comparison with a left-handed dagger.

A position for fencing with the rapier in the right hand and the buckler in the left.

THE ROLE OF THE DAGGER IN MAN-TO-MAN COMBAT

The fencer parries his opponent's rapier with a dagger and immediately attacks with his own rapier.

The combatants clash with the hilts of their rapiers, while the faster of the two successfully attacks with his dagger.

the late sixteenth century. Several types of dagger were designed for this form of sword play and such weapons are called left hand or *main gauche* daggers.

An important accessory to the armour had always been a shield. The knight carried it on his left arm and tried to ward off his opponent's blows, while at the same time attacking with the sword held in his right hand. As late as 1536, the fencing master Marozzo gives an example of how to hold the sword and how the buckler. It was literally only a buckler—made of tough cow hide with a hollow for the fist. The handle of the buckler was fixed with four rivets with large metal heads. The buckler was about 26 cm in diameter. (A small shield of this kind is in the property of the Military History Museum in Prague.) If the fighter broke the blade of his sword he was at the mercy of his opponent and in those days there was not much room for mercy when one was fighting.

The buckler, which was solely a defensive weapon, was replaced by a solid dagger held in the left hand, which could be used quite effectively to parry the opponent's rapier; if the blade of one's own rapier broke or even if the weapon had been knocked out of one's hand, the dagger could be used for attacking.

The dagger was held in the left hand with only the thumb extending over the cross-guard and resting on the blade to give more mastery in the wielding of the weapon. The positions of the hand and the method of combat with a dagger were described in fencing instruction books, generally including illustrations, of the period. One principle was always stressed: the parrying of the opponent's rapier had to be followed immediately by one's own attack. Some daggers were designed in such a way that they could be used not only to parry the opponent's blade but, if wielded by a skilful hand, even to break it.

The dagger, however, was also used in man-to-man combat on its own. In that case the combatants usually held the dagger with the blade pointing downwards. The weapon was then gripped with the whole hand. In pictures of such dagger contests we can often see also the manner in which the opponent's arm was held—they were the same kind of holds as in the Japanese art of self-defence known as *jiu-jitsu*.

As far as the shape of the blade is concerned, one could say that the larger daggers had blades similar in width and thickness to the blades of rapiers. The smaller daggers often had blades of triangular or quadrangular cross-section. There were also very small daggers with beautifully ornamented hilts meant for self-defence. A dagger with a narrow blade is usually known as a *stiletto*.

An interesting type of *stiletto* was the artilleryman's dagger, which had a dual purpose blade: it could be used not only for fighting but also for measuring the calibre of the gun. For this latter purpose the blade had lines indicating the weights of iron, lead or stone cannon balls. With the aid of this the correct amount of gun powder could be measured.

THE CUT AND THRUST WEAPON AS A MUSEUM AND COLLECTOR'S PIECE

In its heyday, the cut and thrust weapon was a dangerous one, especially in the hands of a trained horseman who, with cuts on either side of the neck of his galloping horse, created a large danger area for his enemies. The technological advances of our day have made the cut and thrust weapon obsolete but years, perhaps hundreds of years, after the fame of the shining blade has died away, the weapon appears on our table as a museum or collector's piece awaiting classification and description.

For the sake of simplicity I will use the term 'museum' piece, although I have in mind also the private individual who not only collects weapons but also preserves them and is often an expert in the field. Everybody, however, has to start at some point, and it is my intention to try to introduce the beginner to this very complex collector's field. There is nothing to be lost if the private collector works basically in the same way as the museum expert, on the contrary it can only make his own efforts as a collector more efficient.

Each piece has to be described and classified according to its characteristic features in such a way that not only the type of weapon can be identified but also each individual piece; for this purpose the description is usually supplemented with a sketch or photograph. A good inventory is the basis of a good collection. A special index card may be used for the description and when this is completed the item is entered in the inventory. The index cards used in museums are usually standardized with printed headings. For the private collector, sheets of thin cardboard about 21 × 15 cm in size, on which it is possible to type, should be adequate. The size is sufficient for an extensive description of the weapon, for drawing in sketches, or for the attaching of a photograph. If both sides of one card are not sufficient (which might happen, for instance, when one is describing a weapon with elaborate ornamentation), a second card can be used and this is then fixed to the first.

Each weapon is given a number which is entered in the inventory on the index card and on the piece itself. A collector's interests may of course include military items other than weapons; if several such objects are obtained from the same source at the same time they could be filed under the same number in a catalogue of new acquisitions. In addition this catalogue could list the manner in which the object was obtained, whether by purchase, gift, inheritance, or exchange (this being the oldest way of acquiring things) or discovery. Museums would also list objects that are deposited only on loan. When a discovery is made perhaps during an excavation, the find should be reported and handed over to a museum together with a sketch of the place where the discovery was made. A find of this kind may lead to large-scale discoveries and an inexperienced person should not try to carry out an investigation on his own but rather hand it over to archeologists and take pride in the fact that he has opened up the way to new knowledge.

The description of the new weapon should not be made until the object has been properly cleaned and preserved. Often we come across an excavated weapon that is so corroded that many of its details can be discovered only after the rust has been removed, and these may be important for the correct classification of the weapon. However, if the rust is very thick you should not attempt to do this yourself! Try to get an expert to do this, for although there are many ways in which rust can be removed, one needs a properly equipped laboratory with earthenware tanks large enough to take the whole weapon, and acids, alkalis, hot water, a drying room and chemicals for preserving the cleaned weapon, etc. Inexpert cleaning and preservation of a weapon can completely ruin it. This is true primarily of older weapons; after chemical cleaning an otherwise well-preserved weapon will lose its metal shine and take on a tinned look. With weapons of a more recent date that were in use several decades ago and that have been cleaned regularly with a polish or fine emery, we can use the same materials, at least for small areas of surface rust.

The concise yet graphic description of the weapon is made not only for scientific purposes but also because in case of loss it enables a search to be made, and ensures that when found the weapon can be easily identified. For this reason it is advisable for the index card to be supplied with a photograph or clear sketch of the weapon. The photo should be taken from such an angle that the weapon will not cast a shadow which might distort its shape. Ideally, and certainly with rare items, the photograph should be in colour. When a sketch is made it is better to use diluted Indian-ink or water-colours rather than shading. In practice, of course, the manner in which the sketch is made will depend on one's proficiency.

If the collector is also keeping an inventory and a catalogue of new acquisitions he should write the inventory number in large figures in the card's upper left-hand corner, and the acquisition number in the upper right-hand corner. The inventory can be organized according to one's own interests, giving due consideration to objective factors such as predominance of a certain type of weapon in one's collection. The filing system can be organized with reference to the type of weapon, their place of origin (German weapons, French weapons, etc.), their age and artistic design (especially if we are interested in weapons from a certain historical period). With the help of file-markers or cross-references a combination of several aspects can be used for the organization of the filing system. Given the size of most private collections, using punch cards, the international decimal filing system or modified versions of it would be inappropriate.

All these administrative measures, which might seem tedious at first, are meaningful not only for the obvious practical reasons but mainly because they encourage the collector to become acquainted with his hobby in detail. Even if it is only a hobby—and it is rare, but very satisfying for a hobby to become one's profession—a professional approach to one's own collection adds tremendous enrichment to one's life.

Precision in classifying a weapon lies in placing it in the correct category, such as the type of soldier who used it (infantry, heavy cavalry and so on), country of origin and date. We can also classify it according to the place where it was produced, the maker, the site of its discovery and name of its former user (not owner, unless he also happened to be the one who used it).

The classification of the weapon should be, where possible, supplemented with the source by which it was identified, whether it be a military regulation, an expert treatise, a painting or other work of art showing the weapon (with the author, name of the work and place where it is kept and perhaps the mark under which it is filed), and so on. When we use more than one source, for instance a precisely dated picture and an expert treatise, and find that the two sources differ in the date they give, both the dates with their sources should be listed; of course more than one source can be quoted even in cases where they are in agreement.

Often we are confronted with a weapon about which we are unable to find any exact information. Rather than leave the weapon undescribed we will file an index card with a provisional, general type of description, which can be replaced as soon as a proper classification of the weapon is found. For instance: 'An eleventh-century sword'; 'An ornamental eleventh-century sword'; 'A seventh-century Swedish sword'. In the case of a more modern weapon we might use the following: 'A German-type cavalry sabre from about the second quarter of the nineteenth century'; 'An officer's sword of an unknown type from about the middle of the nineteenth century', and so on.

Sometimes a hypothesis about the origin of the weapon can be formed on the basis of its ornamentation and inscriptions; such a hypothesis must be based on references to comparable material. Furthermore one should not make any inferences without having some well-considered reasons for them and without having a certain basic knowledge. Thus we might have a seventeenth-century rapier whose blade is marked as being made in Toledo but it would be incorrect to conclude that the rapier was necessarily a Spanish one. Toledo blades were, because of their outstanding quality, widespread outside Spanish territory. The entry would therefore run: 'A seventeenth-century rapier with a Toledo blade'. Only if the hilt also carried marks of Spanish origin —a typical rapier of 'Spanish origin' would have a deep bell-basket, long quillons and a simple knuckle bow —could we call it a Spanish rapier.

If the weapon was remarkable for its artistic working the note might read: 'A seventeenth-century ceremonial rapier' or 'An elaborate rapier with a Toledo blade'. Weapons bearing the mark or name of one of the well known master swordsmiths may be classified as follows: 'A rapier with an Antonio Piccinino blade from the end of the sixteenth century'.

A weapon can also be classified by means of the style that gives it its characteristic features, for instance: 'A Romanesque sword', 'A Gothic sword', 'A Renaissance sword', 'A Baroque rapier', 'A Rococo sword'—in the last case it should be made clear whether we are dealing with a ceremonial weapon or a sword whose shape by that time was to some extent determined by military regulations. In the latter case we might write: 'A French officer's sword'. With older weapons such a designation may be used only if we are quite sure that the sword was made and used in that particular country.

In certain cases of weapons of a definite national type it is sufficient to put for instance: 'Claymore from the end of the fifteenth century', in place of: 'A Scottish sword—a claymore from the end of the fifteenth century'; the same would go for the Venetian 'Schiavona' broadsword or the Russian regional 'Shashka' sabre.

A weapon whose shape was determined by military regulations with a designation for a definite type of soldier can be classified as follows: 'A broadsword for the Austrian heavy cavalry dating from 1769', or briefly: 'An Austrian broadsword, model 1769'; as the regulations for that year state that the weapon is to be used by cuirassiers, dragoons and cavalry, whereas the sabre was used only by the Hussars and later on also by the Uhlans.

We can be even more precise in defining a weapon such as a sabre that is clearly a typically Hungarian hussar sabre, and furthermore has the Hungarian emblem engraved on one side of the blade and the name of the commander of the regiment on the other. By referring to the literature we can determine when the weapon came into use and what campaigns the regiment took part in.

If we are lucky enough to own a weapon that belonged to a famous historical figure, the entry on the card would read: 'The sabre of General So-and-so'; a concise biography of the person should also be added. If the former user of the weapon was not an important historical figure, the weapon is classified according to its type; at the end of the description it is mentioned in what function the weapon was used, in what circumstances and by whom. For the private collector the former owner is surely an important person, and he can add this name to the description of the weapon.

Weapons found on the battlefield are usually battered, broken, rusted and so on. Such weapons should not be restored but only preserved so that they do not deteriorate further. These weapons are not only of regional but often also of national interest, depending on the historical importance of the battle in question. A definition of such a weapon might run as follows:

'An Austrian sabre, model 1861 from the battlefield of Hradec Králové.' There are, of course, places where more than one historical battle took place, and though one of them usually predominates in importance, it should be borne in mind that not all the weapons found in this spot are relics from the famous battle.

There are also weapons that bear the name of the battlefield and the date of the battle, for instance: 'Leipzig October 16, 1813'; in the Military History Museum in Prague there is the sabre of Count Franz Schlick which has the names of thirty battlefields from 1809 to 1859 engraved on its scabbard.

There are also weapons that differ fundamentally from the usual models, having a combination of various blades and hilts. These tend to be officer's sabres: to the prescribed hilt a better blade is fixed. The Military History Museum in Prague has in its collections an Austrian infantry sword and a cavalry officer's sabre, both with regulation hilts, but fitted with oriental blades made of excellent material and very light. It also has an Austrian naval officer's sabre with a blade from a Japanese samurai sword. In such a case one might write the following: 'An Austrian cavalry officer's sabre from 1845 with an oriental blade'.

What has just been said is true of weapons that have fairly recent hilts but much older, and generally much better, blades made by one of the well known blade-makers. Of course one has to beware of forgeries usually made to fool collectors who are in the clutches of this interesting but demanding hobby. As a rule, an older hilt will be fixed to a much more recent blade.

Fakes may be found among Renaissance rapiers from the seventeenth century onwards, owing to the richness of the shape of the basket hilts of this period. Often the baskets are cast, which is easily recognizable by the weight and also by the fact that there is usually a clear line where the edges of the mould met. The blade as often as not will not have its characteristic cross-section (seventeenth-century blades often varied in cross-section, the upper part having, say, a cross-section of a flattened hexagonal whereas in the lower part the blade might be rhomboid in cross-section).

In the past, a non-expert collector might have had a whole armoury of such rubbish, for which he had perhaps paid a considerable sum of money. Then in a moment of charity, he might have donated the whole collection to a museum. A gift of such kind from an important person is often more trouble than it is worth—one cannot easily refuse it and so the valueless weapons make their way into the depository of the museum.

While on the subject of forgeries it is worth mentioning at least one other interesting case: a less well-known blade-maker used to mark his products with the name of one of the famous blade-makers. Time passed, until a hundred and fifty years later one of his forged blades acquired a new Baroque hilt. The two incompatible parts were used jointly during the eighteenth century. In such a case we can hardly talk of a forgery for in its own way the weapon is a rarity and as such is of interest to the collector. (In the collection of the Prague National Museum there is a rapier—inventory number 692—of this kind; to give the nameless forger his due the blade in question—purporting to be from the workshop of Antonio Piccinino who lived in Milan from 1509 to 1589—is of very good quality.)

When reconstructions of old weapons are made, the name of the maker and of the person who made the sketch should be listed on the index card. Copies of weapons should be expressly labelled as such, together with the name of the maker. With casts made of plastic we of course do not have to be so careful as it is virtually impossible for them to mislead anyone.

Each weapon should be described in a certain given order: first the blade, then the hilt, hand-guard, length and weight of the weapon, possibly the scabbard and finally the references and our own findings and hypotheses.

THE BLADE

The first part of the weapon to be described is the blade, being the main component of the cut and thrust weapon. It usually has two side faces (unless it is triangular or quadrangular in cross-section), a sharp edge and a back edge, or alternately two sharp edges, a point and a tang to which the grip is attached. If there is a grip, the tang is not mentioned in the description; it is described only if the grip has been ruined by the passage of time so that only the quillons or basket and pommel remain or even only the blade itself.

Firstly the shape of the blade is given—whether it is straight or curved, has only one sharp edge or two and whether it is multi-sided. Now follows the length and width of the blade. For a straight blade the length is measured down the middle from the point to the cross-guard or hilt. For a blade without a hilt or grip the length is also given with the tang included. In the case of curved blades the length is measured in a direct line from the cross-guard or basket to the point. Larger curves should be described by giving the extent of the curve; this is done by measuring the height of the perpendicular from a line drawn from the point to the lower side of the cross-guard on the back edge of the blade and to the highest point of the curve; the perpendicular is measured only to the back edge and not across the sword to the sharp edge. The width of the blade is measured a few centimetres below the cross-guard. If it varies noticeably, for instance towards the point, the width should also be measured there.

In the case of curved blades it is not necessary to mention the sharp edge, because it normally has only one on the outer side of the curve (one exception to this is the Russian kindjhal used by the Tsarist army service corps which had two sharp edges). On some blades, especially curved ones, there is also a sharp edge running from the point for a length of 20-30 cm along the back edge of the weapon; this makes it possible to cut and thrust with the back edge of the weapon if there is no chance of taking a fresh swing and cutting in the usual manner. In certain Austrian broadswords and sabres of the eighteenth century one finds a sharp triangular indentation about 2-3 cm from the point, which presumably served to enlarge the wound after a cut with the back edge of the weapon.

The surface of the sides is also of interest; the cross-section is described, and also how the sides are furrowed with channels or grooves, their length and so on. The channels and grooves are designed to lighten the weight of the blade without adversely affecting its strength. Rapier blades sometimes vary in shape in cross-section two or three times.

The technical description of the blade is concluded with the point, by indicating whether it is in the centre or in line with the back edge. One does not find points on the blade edge side of European weapons. If the point is sharpened in a special manner or has an indentation on the back edge, such details must be noted.

It is important to record the ornamentation of the blade, which may include designs, inscriptions, the names of rulers, military leaders, the rulers' monograms, slogans and sayings. We are also interested in the names of the makers, their signs and indications of the place of manufacture. In the case of more modern blades we must not forget the registration mark of the army, even sometimes the regiment in which the weapon was used. However, these numbers are usually found on the baskets or hilts of the weapon.

When describing the decoration, the type should be indicated, i.e. whether it is exclusively a foliage or floral design, or is combined with other motifs; whether parts of the human body or whole figures are shown, how they are dressed, what weapons they carry and how they are held, whether they are on horseback and so on. With the descriptions of figures should also be given the direction in which they are facing. Blades are often also decorated with stylized images of the sun, half-moons and stars, for instance those made by Peter Munich (1595 to 1660), who worked in Solingen. These designs are also to be found on curved Hungarian blades which often have a figure of the Virgin Mary standing on a half-moon, with a halo round her head in the form of rays.

On some blades, mostly from the first half of the eighteenth century, we come across the name of the ruler linked with a greeting, such as *Vivat Carolus VI,* and on the other side the name of the commander: *Vivat Prinz Eugenius.* Such a greeting was sometimes also accorded to the type of regiment: *Vivat Husar.* These inscriptions were usually engraved so that they could be read when the point was facing upwards and were often accompanied by a figure on horseback.

Military trophies, that is several banners, gun barrels or drums and so on, are also sometimes engraved on blades.

On the blades of Austrian broadswords and sabres of older date we find the two-headed Austrian eagle and crown.

Rapiers usually have their inscriptions running along the axis of the blade.

Rulers' monograms, such as E II (Empress Catherine II) or FR (the Prussian King Frederick II), were usually placed so that the coronets above them faced towards the point.

We also find various slogans with pious content, such as: SOLI DEO GLORIA (Johannes Wundes, 1560-1620), LIVERA (sic) ME DOMINE DE INIMICES MEIS (Hortuno de Aguire, 1606), SI DEUS PRO NOBIS, QUIS CONTRA NOS, or some such soldierly philosophy as: INTER ARMA SILENT LEGES.

Often the slogans were political and patriotic, sometimes linked with a religious theme. From the beginning of the eighteenth century one usually finds the slogan PRO DEO, FIDE ET PATRIA engraved on the blade. In this slogan one can positively feel the danger from Turkey that threatened the heart of Europe. Patriotic slogans with a political content can be found on some Polish sabres from the end of the eighteenth century, for instance: NAROD Z KRÓLEM, KRÓL Z NARODEM (The Nation with the King, the King with the Nation) or simply: HONOR I OJCZYZNA (Honour and Country), a slogan that one could come across even in the twentieth century.

This is just an example of the inscriptions found on blades; sometimes they are light-hearted, often with a touch of sold-ierly black humour.

Another important factor for determining the classification of the blade is the presence of the blade-maker's sign, the maker's name or occasionally a combination of the two. Frequently only the place of production is marked on the blade, e.g. ME FECIT SOLINGEN. The blade-maker's signs were usually stamped in the grooves of the blade or on the ricasso. The dies for stamping the marks became worn fairly quickly and frequently had to be renewed, which led to various small changes in the patterns.

Engraved signs were often inlaid with brass as were also the inscriptions and names. This applies particularly to the famous 'running' or 'Passau wolf' signs. Although as time passed the signs changed to such an extent that one could hardly recognize the original wolf, the term is still used when describing a weapon with such a mark. The mark of the wolf is found on the blades of the Passau blade-makers or those that were produced for the needs of the Passau mercenaries. It was also used in Solingen. The sign was occasionally accompanied by a number, such as '1414' or '1484', and so on—these numbers must not be read as dates!

It is a tremendous help if the place of production is combined with a date, as for example: ME FECIT POTSDAM 1740. With the help of this date we can, by means of comparison, determine the origin of other similar types of blades.

On Toledo blades the letters E and D were marked in a somewhat unusual manner. The special sign was the same in both cases, but differently orientated. If one was not aware of this fact one would read instead of: EN TOLEDO only: N TOL O, as can be seen from the illustration.

The makers of sabre and broadsword blades usually put their names on the back edge of the blades. This was always done in the case of French service weapons. Here are some examples: 'M^{fture} Imp^{le} (= Manufacture Impériale) du Klingenthal Mai 1812'; 'Manuf^{re} R^{le} (= Manufacture Royale) du Klingenthal

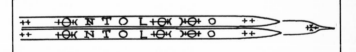

The markings of a Toledo blade dating from the 18th century (Szendrei: Ungarische kriegsgeschichtliche Denkmäler).

Janvier 1815'; 'Mre Imp^{ale} de 'Chât' Janvier 1860 = Carab^{er} Mle 1854 (Chât = Châtellerault, Carab^{er} = Carabinier, Mle = Modèle); 'M^{re} d'Armes de Chât. Février 1883 = Cav^{rie} Légère Mle 1882' (Cav^{rie} = Cavallerie); 'M^{re} d'Armes de Châtt. Juin 1878 = Cav^{rie} L^{re} M^{le} 1882' (L^{re} = légère). These inscriptions give the name of the maker and the date of production; on later types we also find the number of the model and the type of regiment.

The inscriptions on many old weapons are impossible to decipher, however, in spite of all our efforts.

In the description of the blade, as of the other parts of the weapon, we always start with the outer side in so far as it differs from the inner one. The outer side is that side which lies to the right of the person holding the weapon when the sword is drawn with the point upwards and the blade to the fore; when the weapon is sheathed on the left-hand side the outer side lies on the left. The other side is known as the inner side. When the sword is completely symmetrical we write: on one side, on the other.

The blade may be divided into three parts, each of which has its special purpose:

the thin end—this is the flattest part of the blade and includes the point. This part is used for the cut and thrust;

the middle—this part of the blade catches the opponent's blows, deflects his blade from the target and so on;

the thick end—this is the strongest part of the blade just below the hilt, on which the opponent's blows are often caught, and which also serves to force his blade from the target.

When giving a description, however, I find it more useful to use such terms as: in the upper third or lower third, 25 cm from the hilt, 31 cm above the point, and so on. In this case, when speaking of the upper part, the part just below the hilt is meant.

The grip is usually made of wood and wound round with twisted wire, so that the turns touch one another, or it may be wound with cord (with the turns slightly apart) and then covered with skin stretched over it, so that the surface of the grip is raised in a number of ridges. Use in later weapons is also made of fish skin which is rough and does not slip in the hand. With this type of covering the twisted wire was used more for decoration than from necessity and the wire was wound round the grip with spaced turns.

Some grips were made entirely of metal and even cast in brass, constructed in one piece with the quillons, shells and knuckle bar. Brass grips are often found on the military pattern swords of the eighteenth and nineteenth centuries. On special weapons we also come across ivory or bone grips. The hilts of some fairly recent weapons are even made of plastic.

The grip was usually finished off with a metal pommel to which the end of the tang of the blade was riveted or fixed with a little cap which covered the upper part of the grip and held the upper end of the knuckle guard. The pommel, especially during the eighteenth and nineteenth centuries, was sometimes in the shape of a lion's or eagle's head. At other times the entire back of the grip was protected by a so-called back-rib made of the same material as the hilt. The end of the tang was riveted to the back-rib at its peak. Officers and non-commissioned officers carried broadswords and sabres that also ended in the shape of a lion's or eagle's head.

On Baroque, Rococo and more recent swords the top part of the knuckle bow is fixed to the pommel by means of a knuckle bow hook or knuckle bow screw.

THE HAND-GUARD

The last parts of the weapon to be described are the guards. Where it is a simple bar, straight or S-shaped, either vertically or horizontally, we call it the cross-guard or quillons. These are to be found on medieval swords and on Hungarian sabres of the sixteenth and seventeenth centuries. Mention should also be made of the narrow, perpendicular bars which rest at one end against the grip and at the other hold the sword in its sheath. This part of the cross-guard is called the languet. They are to be found on many broadswords and sabres, and also on hilts of swords of the eighteenth and nineteenth centuries. The angle of the quillons should also be noted and whether they are finished off in any special manner.

If the guard is complex it is referred to as a basket. In this case a description should be given of the material of which it is made, its shape, whether it is a swept, deep complex, or a bell-shaped hilt (typical of the Spanish rapier) and also the type of decoration. The arsenal mark and regimental sign and number should also be recorded. In the case of a rapier the number of guard rings or counter guards should be mentioned and whether they are on the inner or outer side. In the case of deep, cup hilts the number of holes or openings that have been pierced in it should be noted.

The description should be ended by giving the total length and weight of the weapon.

If the weapon has a scabbard this should also be described, stating whether it is made of leather or wood covered with leather or metal, what kind of metal mounts it displays and how it is fixed to the hanging straps. The sabre sheathed in its scabbard, hanging by the soldier's side, gave rise to the term 'side arm'.

As has been pointed out earlier, the description of the weapon ought to be supplemented by references to the literature.

It would clearly also be of great help if the collector tried to get to know the uniforms of the armies in which the weapons of his collection were used. Gradually over the years one can collect a whole range of information, a kind of small private encyclopedia or at least a study aid. Not relying solely on one's own memory, however good it might be, and collecting information of this kind will surely pay in the long run and one's efforts will certainly not be lost.

THE DESCRIPTIONS OF SWORDS
AND DAGGERS

LIST OF ABBREVIATIONS

AWU   Archiv für Waffen- und Uniformkunde (Frankfurt am Main) 1, 1918

Bruhn Hoffmeyer   Ada Bruhn Hoffmeyer: Middelalderens Tvaeggede Svaerd, Copenhagen 1954

Dreger   E. H. Max Dreger: Waffensammlung Dreger, Berlin—Leipzig 1926

Ffoulkes   Charles Ffoulkes: Arms and Armament. A Historical Survey of the Weapons of the British Army, London 1945

Krickel—Lange   G. Krickel—G. Lange: Das deutsche Reichsheer in seiner neuesten Bekleidung und Ausrüstung, Berlin 1889

Laking   F. G. Laking: A Record of European Arms and Armour through Seven Centuries, London 1926

M.   model of weapon

Matějček   Antonín Matějček: Česká malba gotická (Gothic Painting in Bohemia), Prague 1938

MM   Military History Museum in Prague

NM   National Museum in Prague

Rousselot   Lucien Rousselot: L'Armée Française, ses Uniformes, son Armement, son Equipement, Paris 1944

Sammlung Gimbel   Waffen- und Kunstsammlung Karl Gimbel, Baden-Baden 1904

Sammlung Hollitzer   Versteigerungskatalog Sammlung Hollitzer (Kunstauktion 429), Wien 1934

Teuber—Ottenfeld   Oscar Teuber—Rudolf von Ottenfeld: Die österreichische Armee von 1700 bis 1867, Wien 1895

t. l.   total length of weapon

w. d.   without date of publication

w. p.   without place of publication

wt.   weight of weapon

ZHW   Zeitschrift für historische Waffenkunde (Dresden), 1897 to 1899 and others (re-appeared as Zeitschrift für Historische Waffen- und Kostümkunde, 1921/1922 and others).

1 A bronze sword from the period 900—750 BC: Mörigerschwert,
   Gailenkirchen, Württemberg. Herbert Kühn: Die Vorgeschichtliche
   Kunst Deutschlands (Propyläen), Berlin 1935, pp. 300—301.

2 A bronze sword from the period 900—750 BC: Antennenschwert,
   Schussenried, Württemberg. Ibid., pp. 300—301.

3 A reconstruction of a Swedish-type sword of the 7th century. The grip is of gilded bronze. Another example reconstructed by the Swedish archeologist Oskar Montelius (1843—1921), a leading expert on the Bronze Age, has a gilded grip inlaid with silver and garnets. ZHW VIII, pp. 33—34.

3

4　The sword of St Stephen dating from the 9th—10th century. L. of blade 75.5 cm, W. 4 cm. The pommel and quillons are made of ivory. The wire binding of the grip dates from about the 18th century. Eduard Šittler—Antonín Podlaha: Poklad svatovítský. In: Soupis památek historických a uměleckých, Prague 1903, pp. 14—15, Pl. 10—11.

5　A Viking sword of the 9th century, with an ornamented hilt of Frankish origin. Found in Norway. Hans Friedrich Blunk: Die Nordische Welt. In: Propyläen-Weltgeschichte, Berlin w.d., p. 121.

4

5

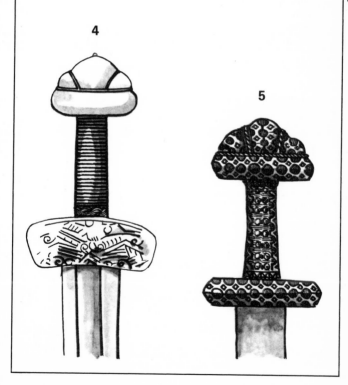

6   A sword from the 10th—11th century. Laking I, p. 15. Pl. 17.

7   A sword from the 11th century. Laking I, p. 15, Pl. 18.

8   A sword from the 11th century. Laking I, p. 15, Pl. 19.

9   A sword from the end of the 12th century; t.l. 91 cm. A similar sword is dated by Bruhn Hoffmeyer (Pl. VI) as from 1175—1200. Owner: NM.

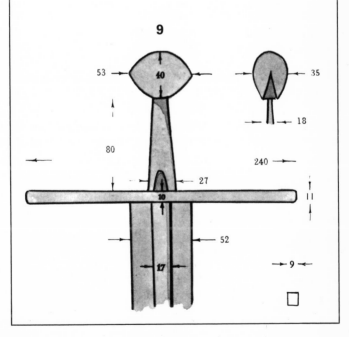

9

10 A knight's sword, probably dating from the end of the 11th century; l. 78.5 cm, w. 5.8 cm. On one side in a broad fuller (2.2 cm) the inscription SIGVINAIS is engraved. The sword has a highly interesting pommel in the shape of a Brazil nut with inlay decoration on either side: on one side there is a stylized tree (representing the Old Testament symbol of man's first sin) and on the other side a fish lying below a fishing net (symbolizing the New Testament, i.e. Christianity and redemption). T.l. 92 cm, wt. 1 kg. Owner: MM.

11 A sword from about the middle of the 13th century. Bruhn Hoffmeyer Pl. XII and XV. Owner: NM.

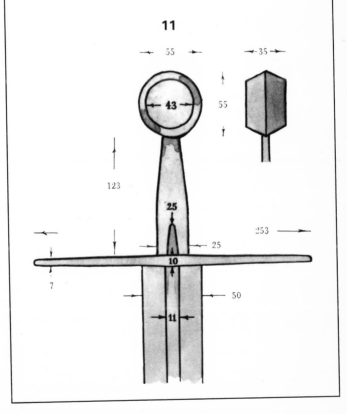

11

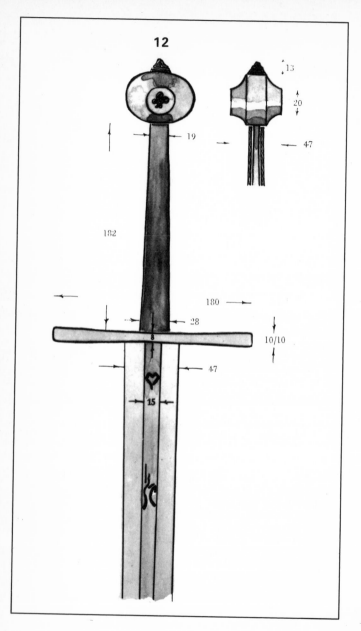

12

12 A sword dating from about 1350—1400. L. of blade 104.5 cm, t.l. 128.2 cm. In the fuller of the blade there is a mark closely resembling the Passau wolf sign. Owner: NM.

13 A sword depicted in the panel-painting by the Master of the Třeboň Altarpiece: The Three Saints, dating from the year 1380. Matějček Pl. 88.

13

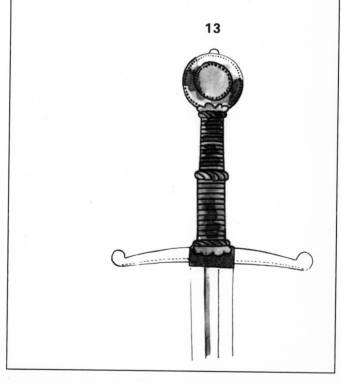

14

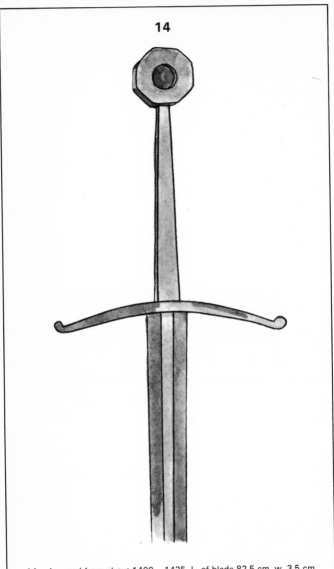

14   A sword from about 1400 —1425. L. of blade 82.5 cm, w. 3.5 cm,
t.l. 105.5 cm. Bruhn Hoffmeyer Pl. XXVI c. Owner: MM.

15

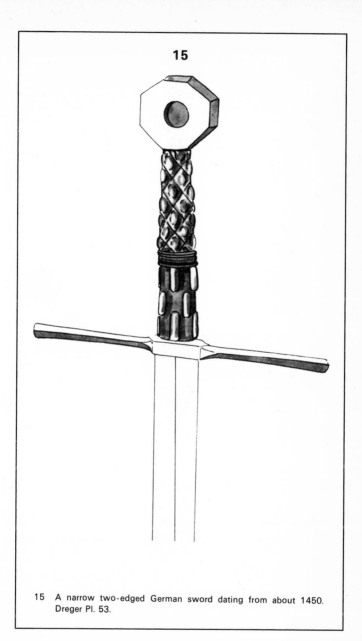

15 A narrow two-edged German sword dating from about 1450.
Dreger Pl. 53.

16

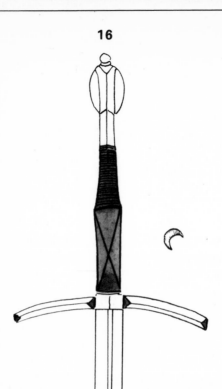

16 A narrow two-edged German sword from around 1480. Dreger
    Pl. 59. A sword with a similar hilt is depicted by A. Dürer in the
    Paumgärtner Altarpiece in Munich. (Curt Glasser: Die Altdeutsche
    Malerei, Munich 1924, Pl. 226).

17 A sword with S-shaped quillons dating from 1436—1450. L. of
    blade 92 cm, t.l. 115.5 cm. Bruhn Hoffmeyer Pl. XXXIV b and
    XXXVIII c. Owner: NM.

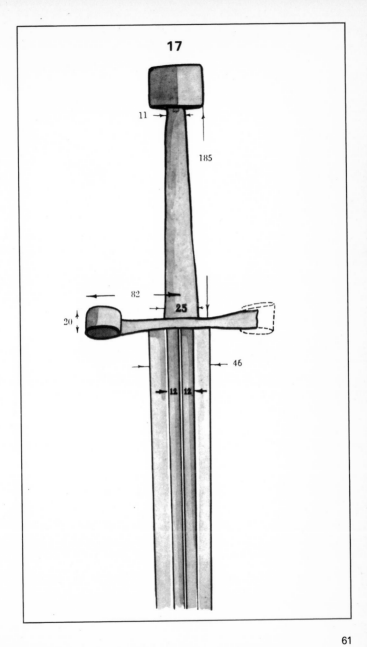

18 A sword from the end of the 15th century with one guard (at the front) for the protection of the forefinger. Laking II, p. 289, Pl. 670.

19 A Spanish sword from the end of the 15th century with two arms of the hilt. Laking II, p. 291, Pl. 673.

18

19

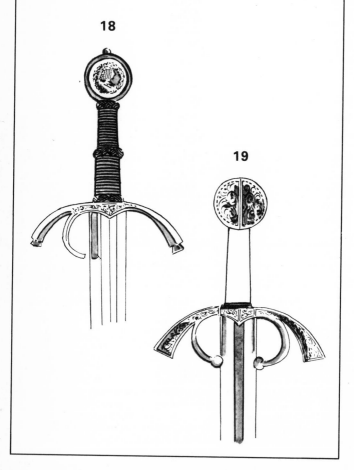

20

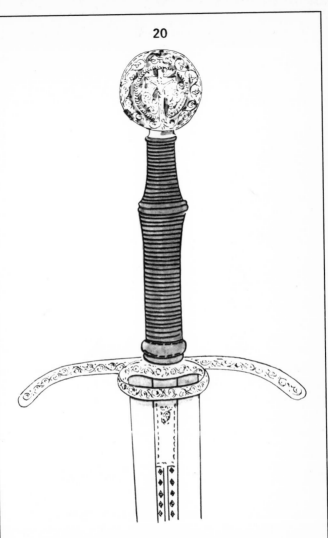

20 A Spanish sword dating from 1475 with a broad two-edged blade
and a one-and-a-half handed grip ending in a pommel with a cruci-
fix. A swordsmith's mark is stamped on the blade just below the
hilt. The quillons have a side ring guard for the protection of the
hand. Dreger Pl. 34, fig. 68.

21 The so-called 'Katzbalger' Landsknecht sword from around 1520.
    Wt. about 1.5 —2 kg. Dreger Pl. 66.

21

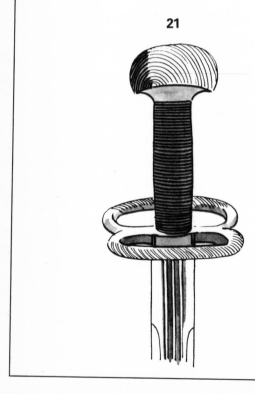

22

22 A sword from the third quarter of the 16th century, whose ring
    guard afforded considerable protection to the hand. Laking IV,
    p. 268, Pl. 1332.

23

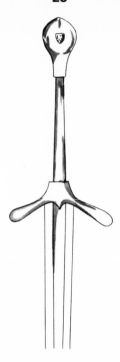

23 A Scottish claymore from the end of the 15th century. Laking II,
p. 305, Pl. 686.
The claymore was the original Scottish two-handed sword of the
15th and 16th centuries with downward drooping quillons. (George
Cameron Stone: A Glossary of the Construction, Decoration and
Use of Arms and Armour, Portland 1934).

24 Two-handed swords, used primarily by the Landsknechts. The
weight of these weapons was from 3.50 to 5.25 kg. Surprisingly
enough they were not difficult to wield. The first two are of German
origin, from *c.* 1570. The length of such swords was about 180 cm,
the length of the grip as much as 45 cm, of the cross-guard about
42 cm. The width of the blade was 3.3 cm. ZHW VIII, p. 200, Pl. 3
shows an Italian sword of this type. Cf. also ZHW I, p. 63, Pl. 1.

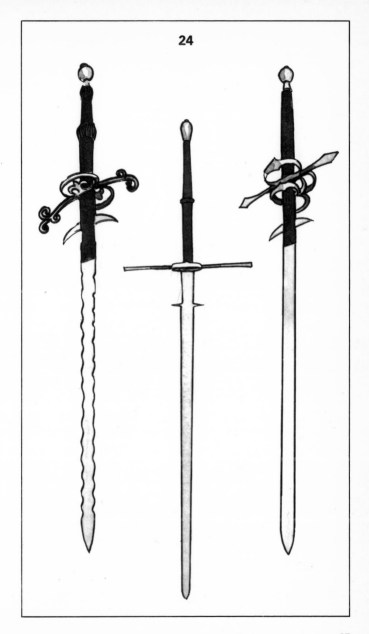

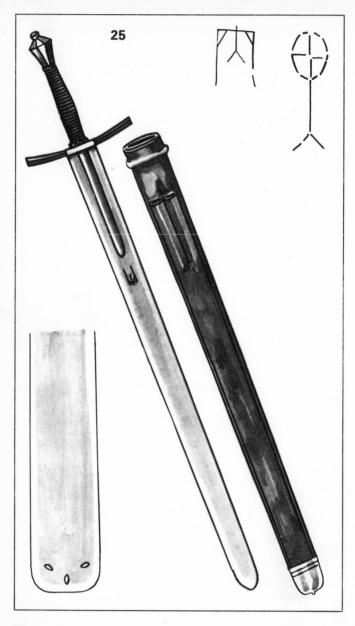

24

25 The executioner's sword. This is strictly speaking an instrument and not a weapon, since it was used solely against a passive person. The blade, usually about 4.5—5.5 cm wide, and 80—85 cm long, had no point. The grip and pommel together were about 21—22 cm. On some specimens the blade was decorated with appropriate symbols of punishment or relevant verses.

26 A rapier from the beginning of the 17th century. The blade is straight, 98 cm long and 2.7 wide. The sword has a fairly simple swept hilt made of steel, with a single outer guard ring from which another counter-guard sweeps up towards the knuckle guard. At the lower end there is a horizontal ring usually but incorrectly known as the *pas d'âne*. On the inner side there is a guard with three arms. T.I. 113 cm, wt. 1.40 kg. Owner: NM.

26

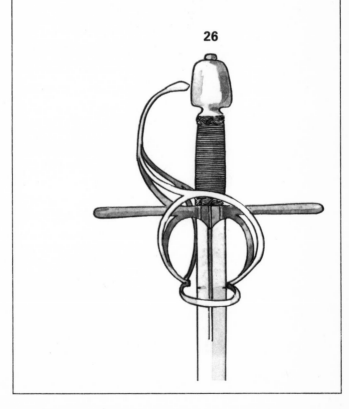

27

27 A rapier from the late 16th or early 17th century. L. of the blade including ricasso 95 cm, w. 2.7 cm. The grip is spirally twisted. The complex basket is made of iron with a straight cross-guard 23.5 cm long. From the bottom of the rear arm a counter-guard sweeps out and round to the front, ending in a stylized serpent's head. T.l. 114 cm. Private collection.

28

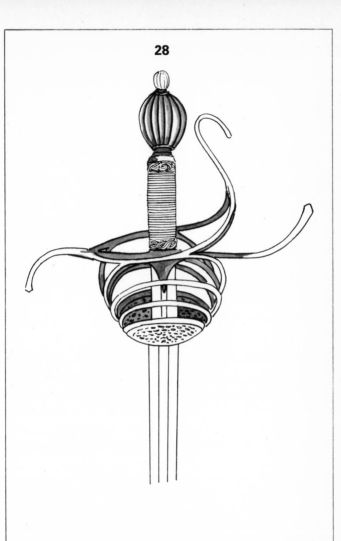

28 A rapier from the end of the 16th century. T.l. 140 cm. The quillons are S-shaped and the front guard is hooked in order to catch the opponent's blade. R. Forrer: Die Waffensammlung des Herrn Stadtrath Richard Zschille in Grossenheim, Berlin 1894, Pl. 137, fig. 343.

29 A slender rapier with a swept hilt with several counter-guards. Dreger classifies this as a German civilian weapon from around 1600. (Pl. 58, fig. 103.)

30 A Flemish rapier from the first quarter of the 17th century. There is no horizontal guard, but a single ring enclosing a perforated metal plate which protects the hand. Laking IV, p. 327.

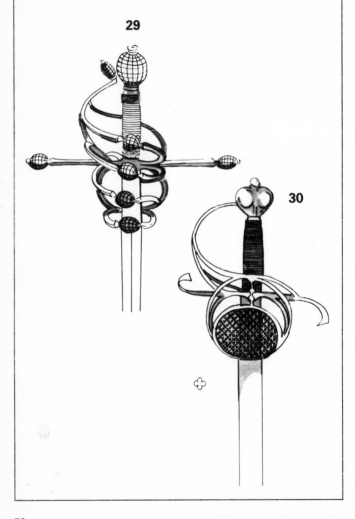

31   A rapier from about 1600, probably a costume sword. The complex
      basket consists of flat ribs and a cross-guard. Dreger Pl. 52,
      fig. 93.

31

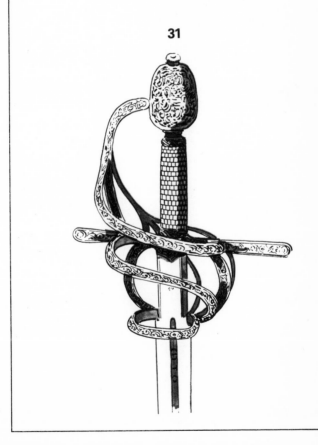

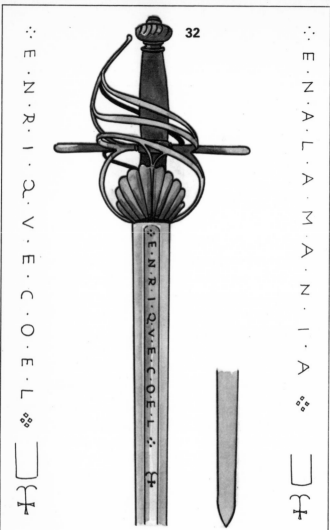

32 A sword from around 1590—1610. It has a straight two-edged blade, 66.5 cm long, and 3.5 cm wide. On the blade is engraved the name of the maker: ENRIQUE COEL and the place of manufacture: EN ALAMANIA. The swept hilt is of steel and asymmetrical. Owner: MM.

33 A sword from the 16th—17th century. The blade is straight, two-edged, 81.5 cm long and 3.6 cm wide, and has two fullers on either side in which the inscription JESUS—MARIA is engraved. The basket is of iron and consists of flat guards and connecting bars. The inscription on the blade JESUS—MARIA was commonly used by Milanese armourers and these names were also used by Luis de Aiala, the son of Thomas Aiala, who worked in Barcelona in 1566—1620. Wendelin Boeheim: Meister der Waffenschmiede-kunst vom XIV. bis ins XVIII. Jahrhundert, Berlin 1897, p. 4.

34 A *Schiavona* sword from the 17th century. This was the sword of the Venetian infantry, which consisted mainly of Dalmatian mercenaries. The blade is straight, either single or double edged, approximately 84 cm long and 3 cm wide. The basket is deep, made up of a number of connecting bars protecting the whole hand. Inside the basket there is a thumb guard. T.l. 97.5 cm, wt. 1.23 kg. Owner: MM.

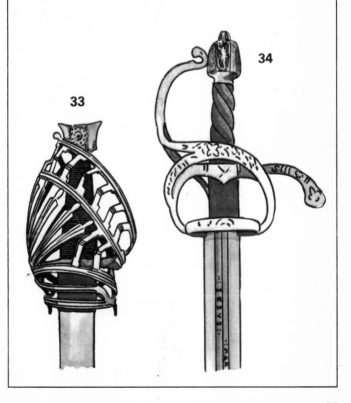

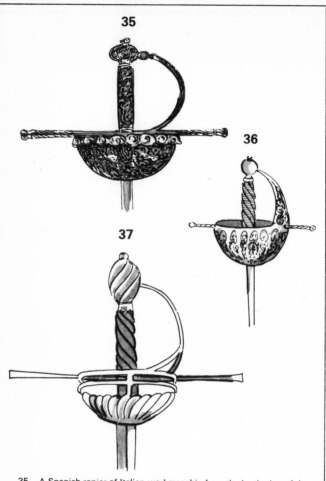

35 A Spanish rapier of Italian workmanship from the beginning of the 17th century. The typical hilt consists of a deep bell-shaped basket, long quillons and a knuckle guard. The basket is richly decorated. Laking V, p. 73, Pl. 1488.

36 A Spanish rapier from around 1630—1640. Laking V, p. 67, Pl. 1480.

37 An English rapier from the beginning of the 17th century. Laking IV, p. 321, Pl. 1384.

38

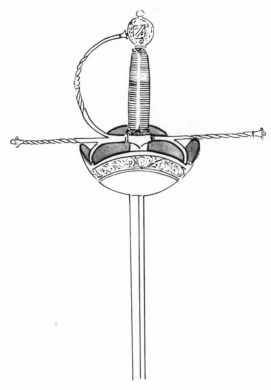

38 A Spanish rapier from the end of the 16th century. Georg Hiltl: Die Waffensammlung Sr. Königlichen Hoheit des Prinzen Carl von Preussen, Berlin w.d., Pl. XXXVIII.

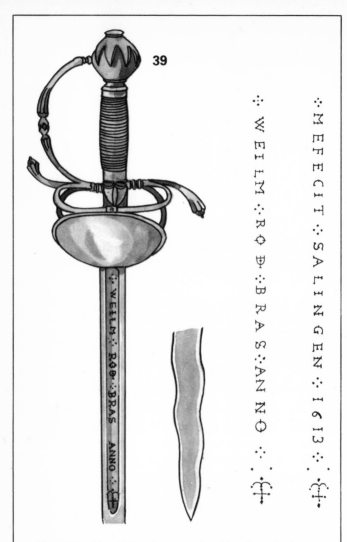

39 A rapier from 1613 with a wavy edge, 94 cm long. On the outer face is the name of the blade-maker: WEILM ROD BRAS ANNO, on the other the remainder of the inscription: ME FECIT SALINGEN 1613. The rapier has an asymmetrical plain shell, supported on the outer side by a horizontal ring guard. Owner: MM.

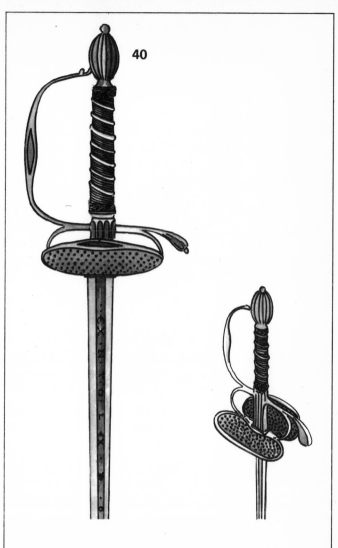

40 A rapier from the second half of the 17th century with a Toledo blade. The blade bears the typical Toledo trade mark — EN TOLEDO — with its special symbols for the letters D and E. L. of blade 97.2 cm. On the hilt are traces of gilding.

41 A 14th-century dagger of Danish origin. ZHW 1929/1931, p. 269. This type of weapon is of course found in other parts of Europe as well. One is in the Municipal Museum of Prague.

42 A French dagger of the 15th century. R. Forrer: Die Waffensammlung des Herrn Stadtrath Richard Zschille in Grossenheim, Berlin 1894, p. 421, Pl. 149.

41 **42**

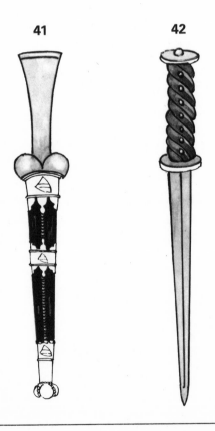

43 A dagger from a knight's belt. Viollet le Duc: Dictionnaire raisonné du mobilier français V, p. 317.

43

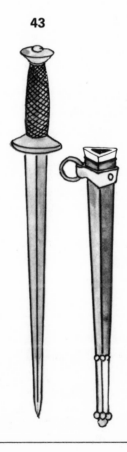

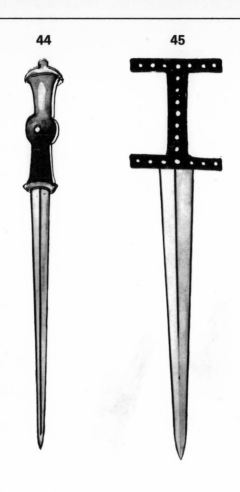

44 **45**

44 An English dagger from 1440. Laking III, p. 21, Pl. 774.

45 A dagger known as the *Baselard,* from the beginning of the 15th century. Laking III, p. 10, Pl. 748. A dagger of this type is to be found on the Czech gothic panel painting called The Kaufmann Crucifixion (after 1350): the bailiff is just about to cut Christ's cloak in half with it (Matějček Pl. 33 and 36).

46   A dagger from the end of the 14th century. Laking III, p. 4, Pl. 729.

47   A dagger from *c.* 1420 with a leather guard beneath the grip. (The Reininghausen Altarpiece, St Magdalene and St Lucia—Matějček Pl. 205).

48   A dagger from about the middle of the 16th century. It has an oval-shaped pommel, straight quillons and an iron ring guard with very fine inlaid silver decoration. T.l. 47.5 cm. The hilt including the quillons is 13 cm long. Sammlung Gimbel, Pl. XIV, fig. 531.

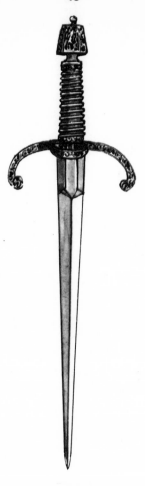

49   A dagger from about the middle of the 16th century; t.l. 38 cm.
The hilt including the quillons is 13.5 cm long. The pommel is ornamented with a human figure and the whole weapon is inlaid with
silver. Sammlung Gimbel, Pl. XIV, fig. 532.

50

50 A dagger with S-shaped quillons. It is depicted on the belt of the
    musketeer. Jacob de Geyn: Waffenhandlung von den Rören,
    Musqueten und Spiessen, Grauenhagen 1608, Pl. 21.

51 A Spanish weapon known as a left-handed dagger and used in
    conjunction with a rapier. It has long quillons with a finely pierced
    curved triangular plate reaching to the pommel, thus protecting the
    whole hand. The blades of such daggers were often reinforced just
    below the hilt so that they could ward off the cuts of the opponent's
    rapier without breaking. Various small additions are often found
    on this part of the blade and were intended to catch the opponent's
    blade. Sammlung Gimbel, Pl. XIX, figs. 548 and 549, gives the
    length of such daggers as 48 cm to 56 cm.

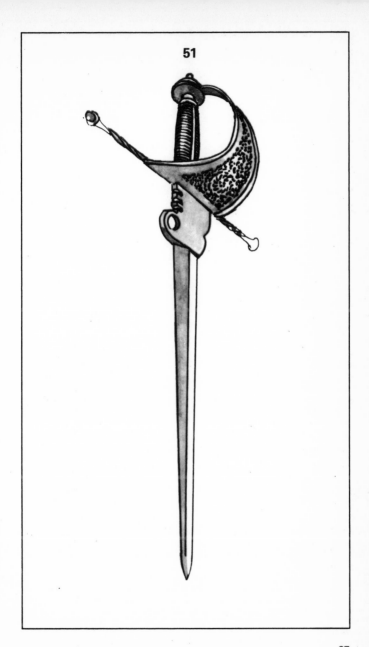

52

52 The dagger known as the *sword breaker*. It has a flat wide blade
    with one of its sides deeply serrated. If the opponent's blade got
    caught in this section the teeth would prevent it from being freed
    and the defender could, with a suitable movement of his hand,
    break his adversary's blade. August Demmin (Die Kriegswaffen in
    ihrer geschichtlichen Entwicklung, Leipzig 1893, p. 768, Pl. 32)
    places this dagger in the 16th century. Owner: Historical Museum
    in Dresden (Zwinger).

53 A dagger with a split blade, from the 16th—17th century. The blade has two side-arms fixed to a rod inside the centre blade with two springs at the base of the blade. When the rod was withdrawn the side arms sprang outwards, positioning themselves against the drooping quillons. This forked dagger could then more easily catch the opponent's blade, or alternatively the blade could be sprung open inside a wound, thus making it much more severe. Owner: NM.

53

54

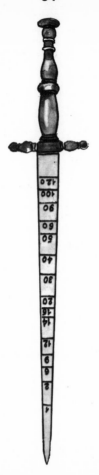

54 An artillery man's *stiletto* from the end of the 17th century. It has
a narrow blade, triangular or quadrangular in cross-section, with
a measuring scale marked on it. It could be used instead of a measuring rod which gave on the various faces the weights of iron,
stone or lead cannon balls. The correct amount of gun powder
could then be chosen according to the weight of the cannon ball.
Frederick Wilkinson: Arms and Armour, London 1971, p. 117.

55 An Italian dagger with a broad blade from the 15th—16th century known as the *cinquedea,* the equivalent of the German *Ochsenzunge.* Its Czech name *veruna* is interesting in that it clearly reminds one of the Italian town Verona. Sammlung Gimbel shows several of these weapons measuring 42, 46, 60 and 63.5 cm. The width of the blade just below the hilt is 7—9 cm, gradually narrowing down towards the point. One usually finds shallow grooves on the blade arranged as follows: four just below the hilt, three more further down, then two and finally a single one. The width of the blade was ideally suitable for decoration and so one often finds here several figures grouped together.

56 A falchion from the beginning of the 14th century with a widening blade that has a straight back edge. Laking I, pp. 128—129, Pl. 157 and 158.

57 St Bartholomew's falchion depicted in the Epitaph of John of Jeřeň dating from 1395. In Gothic paintings martyrs usually carry in their hands the weapon that put an end to their life (Matějček p. 128). This weapon is also held by the executioner of St John the Baptist depicted in the Zátoň Altarpiece dating from 1430 (Matějček p. 218); it is also depicted in the hands of the soldiers guarding the Holy Sepulchre and also as a symbol of guilt on the crosses of the crucified villains. (Curt Glaser: Die altdeutsche Malerei, München 1924, p. 57, Pl. 38). Apparently it was thought of as the weapon of base, dishonourable people.

56

57

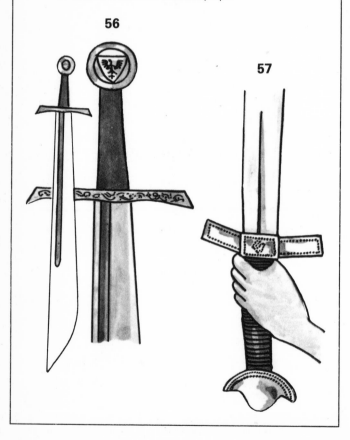

58   A Hungarian sabre from the middle of the 15th century. ZHW
     1935, Pl. 10 following p. 152, No. 8.

58

59

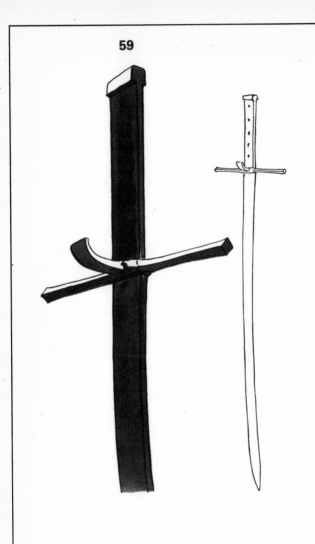

59 A sabre know as the *Hiebmesser*. Originally in the 15th century
it was a burghers' weapon but later on it was also used by knights.
Quirin Leitner: Die Waffensammlung des österreichischen Kaiserhauses im k. k. Artillerie-Arsenal-Museum in Wien, Wien 1866 to
1870, p. 70.

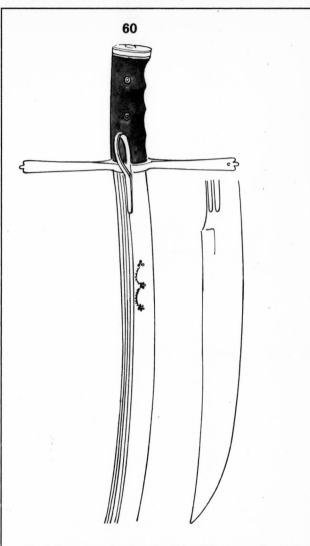

60

60 A Hungarian sabre from the 16th—17th century. The blade is
curved, 80 cm long and 3.2 cm wide, with a 27.3 cm long, two-
edged point. The quillons are 22 cm long with langets on each
side, 10 cm in length. Private collection.

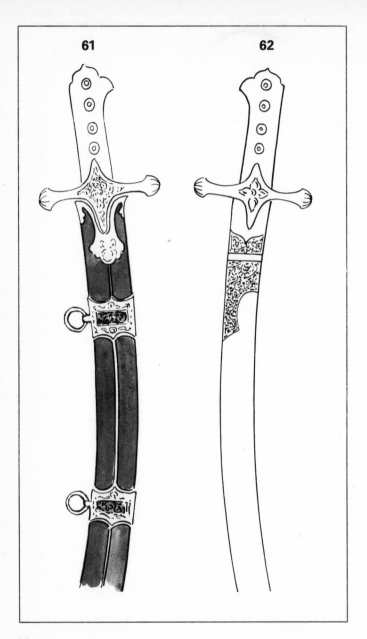

61 A Turkish sabre from the 17th century in its scabbard. The scabbard is covered in rough black leather and is mounted with silver decoration. Owner: MM.

62 The same weapon without its scabbard. The blade is curved and inlaid with silver. The grip is of white bone and the quillons and langets are decorated. Owner: MM.

63 A Polish *Karabela* sabre from the 17th century. It has a very broad curved blade. The hilt is of dark horn with engraved arrows pointing upwards. The quillons are fairly short with both arms drooping. The metalwork on the scabbard is usually in silver or brass. Wendelin Boeheim: Handbuch der Waffenkunde, Leipzig 1890, p. 278, Pl. 317. Owner of a similar weapon: MM.

63

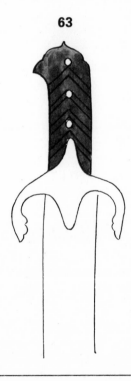

64

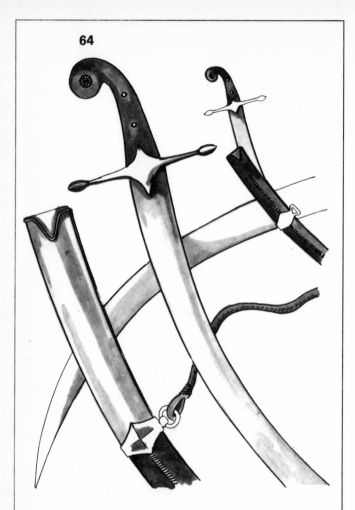

64 A Turkish *Kilij* from the 18th century. It has a sharply curved blade
which was usually ornamented with Oriental designs and quota-
tions from the Koran, sometimes in gold. The hilt usually had a grip
of dark horn and a pommel which curled towards the front. Owing
to the sharp curve of the blade the scabbard was usually slit down
the upper third so that the weapon could be easily drawn. Wendelin
Boeheim: Handbuch der Waffenkunde, Leipzig 1890, p. 275, Pl.
314.

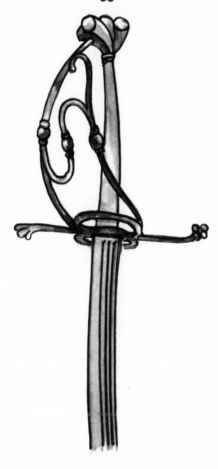

65 A Swiss sabre from between 1530—1540. It has a relatively long grip and a fairly simple hilt, consisting of quillons with two side rings; an inner and outer rib sweeping upwards from the quillons are joined together by an S-shaped counter-guard. Eduard Wagner: Cut and Thrust Weapons, London 1967, p. 314 — according to ZHW 6, p. 304, Pl. 24 —25.

66 A sabre from the borders of Austria and Hungary, known as the *Bauernwehr* which was in use at the turn of the 16th and 17th century. The blade is Hungarian, slightly curved and of the same type as that used by the hussars. The basket is German and varied in design. Of interest is the type where a triangular metal plate extends from the cross-guard up towards the pommel. Owner: MM.

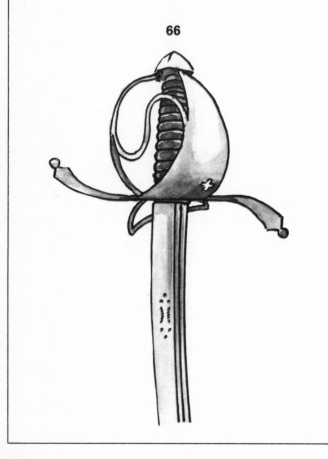

66

67

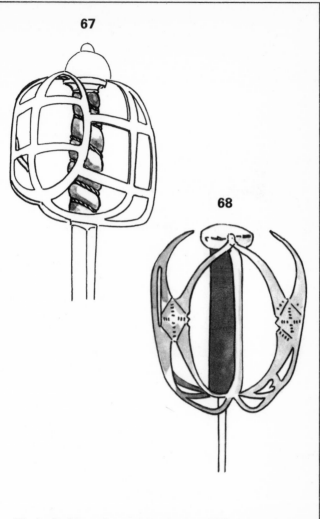

68

67 An English cavalry trooper's sabre from 1705. It has a latticed basket, protecting the whole hand. Ffoulkes, p. 39, Pl. 34 (A).

68 An English cavalry trooper's sabre from 1751; the massive hilt reminds one of a typical Scottish broadsword. Ffoulkes, p. 39, Pl. 34 (B).

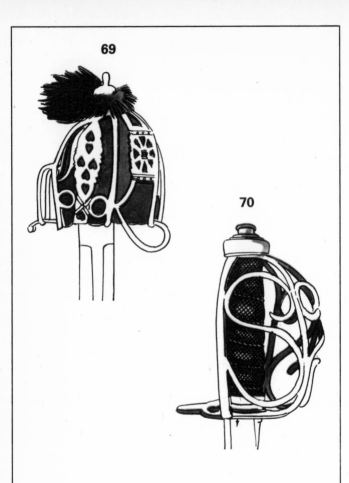

69 A Scottish broadsword from the first half of the 20th century. Ffoulkes, p. 43, Pl. 36 (C). Howard L. Blackmore: Arms and Armour, London 1965, pp. 118—119. Swords of this type were in use as early as the late 16th century.

70 An English grenadier private's sword from 1751. It has four rings joined by S-shaped bars. Ffoulkes, p. 43, Pl. 36 (B).

71

71 A sword of the English royal dragoons from 1788. Ffoulkes, p. 37,
    Pl. 31 (C). .

72 A Bavarian cuirassier's broadsword from 1700. The blade is
    straight, one-edged, with a central point. On the outer side is the
    slogan: PRO DEO, FIDE ET PATRIA; on the inner side: VIVAT.
    The grip is covered with leather and ends in an iron cap narrowed
    to a beak in the front. The hilt is of iron, with a front knuckle guard
    and three irregular counter-guard bars. On the inner side there is
    a thumb guard. The scabbard is of wood, covered with leather and
    iron mounts. Sammlung Hollitzer, Pl. XXVII, fig. 310.

72

73 An Austrian cavalry broadsword from the last quarter of the 17th century. The blade is straight and two-edged, the iron hilt has two knuckle bows joined by a counter-guard. On the inner side there is a thumb ring. Owner: MM.

73

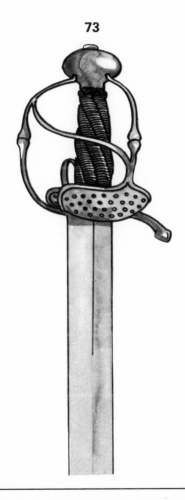

74 A Saxony dragoon's sabre from the end of the 18th century. The blade is slightly curved, 91.3 cm long and 3 cm broad. Beneath the hilt there is the monogram FA with a coronet. The grip is wound with twisted wire and has an iron pommel. The iron hilt is made up of bands that unite with the front knuckle bow. T.l. 107 cm, wt. 1.38 kg. The scabbard is of wood covered with leather and with brass mounts. Sammlung Hollitzer, Pl. XXVIII, fig. 338.

74

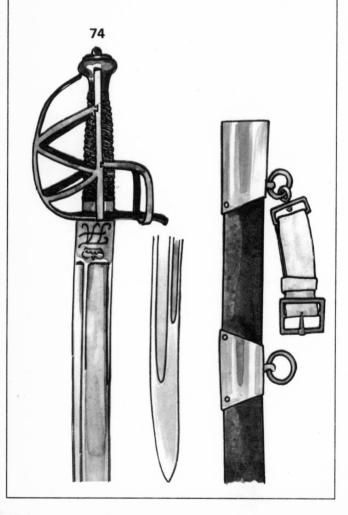

75　A Prussian cuirassier's broadsword, M. 1732 from the time of Frederick II. The blade is straight, two-edged, 94.3 cm long and 4.3 cm wide. A small eagle is stamped on the outer side and on the inner side is the inscription: POTZDAM. The grip is covered with leather and has a brass egg-shaped pommel. The hilt has a brass guard with an eagle bearing the monogram FR on its breast on the outer side. T.l. 110.3 cm. Owner: MM.

75

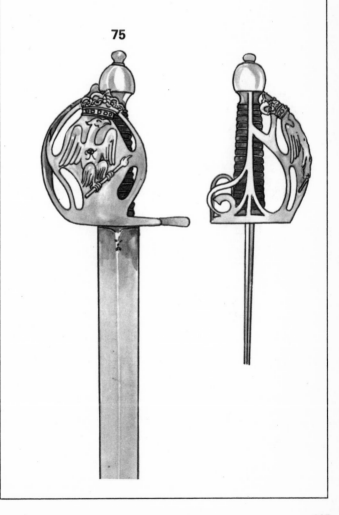

76

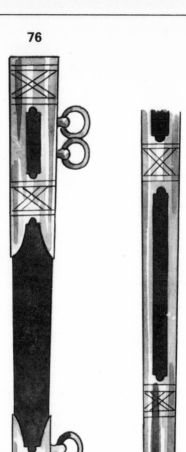

76 The scabbard of the previous broadsword. It is of wood, covered
with leather, with iron mounts which are pierced with long slots.
Owner: MM.

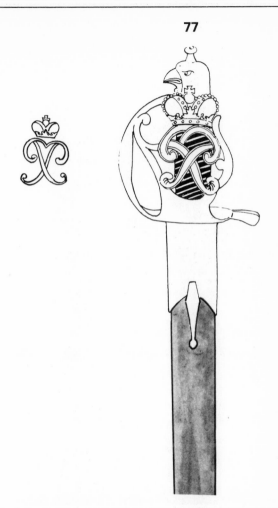

77 A Russian dragoon's broadsword from the years 1756—1762. It
resembles the Prussian cuirassier broadsword of the same period
both in the shape of its hilt and the metal mounts of the scabbard,
excluding the suspension lug. The pommel of the sword is in the
shape of an eagle's head. A. V. Viskovatov: Istoricheskoe opisaniye odiezhdy i vooruzheniya rossiyskikh voysk, St Petersburg
1899, III, Pl. 444 and 456.

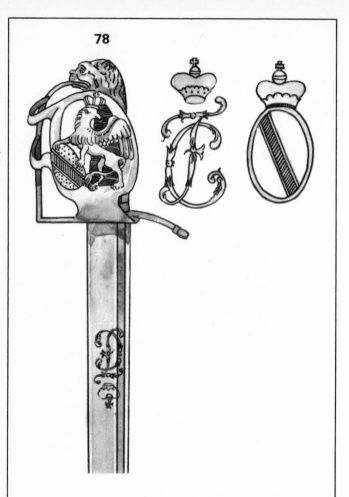

78

78 A Baden dragoon's broadsword from the beginning of the 19th century. It has a straight single-edged blade, 88 cm long, 3.8 cm wide. On the outer side the monogram CF is engraved, on the inner side the emblem of Baden in an oval beneath a duke's coronet. The grip, which is covered in leather, has a brass back rib ending in a lion's head. The hilt is of brass with a guard plate bearing the Baden emblem. T.l. 102 cm, wt. 1.35 kg. Sammlung Prof. Louis Braun, Waffen und Uniformen von 16. Jahrhundert, insbesondere der Napoleonischen Zeit, München 1914, Pl. 10, fig. 112.

79   A sabre of Saxony's Kurfürst cuirassier regiment from the years
1799—1800. The blade is slightly curved, 93.5 cm long and 3.3
cm wide. The grip is covered with leather and ends in a lion's head.
The hilt is of brass, with a guard plate rising in an arc and the monogram FA embossed upon it. T.l. 109.5 cm, wt. 1.27 kg. The
scabbard is made of leather. AWU, vol. I, Pl. 7.

79

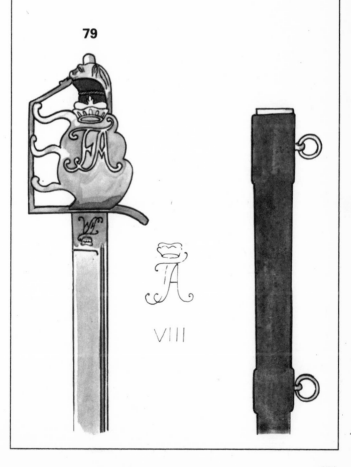

80 An Austrian cavalry broadsword from about 1763. The blade is straight, with a back-edge point. The hilt is of brass. The guard plate is connected with the knuckle bow by three counter-guards. On the inner side there is a thumb ring with a short counter-guard. Owner: MM.

80

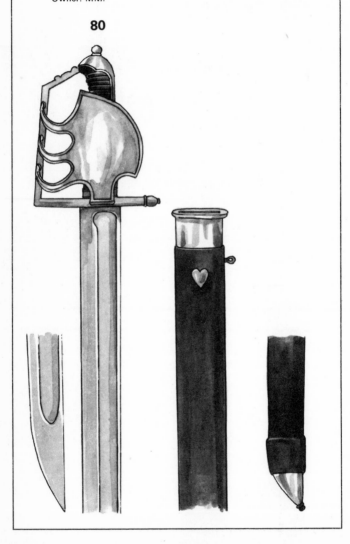

81

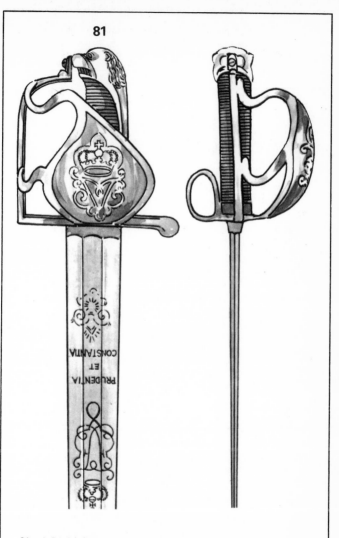

81 A Danish heavy cavalry broadsword, M. 1705. The straight two-edged blade is 84.6 cm long and 3.7 cm wide. The grip has a brass back rib ending in a lion's head. A guard plate with two counterguards is on the inner side of the brass hilt bearing the royal monogram and coronet. T.l. 98.3 cm, wt. 1.11 kg. Owner: MM.

82 An Austrian heavy cavalry broadsword from the first half of the 18th century. The blade is straight, single-edged, and decorated with a figure of a rider and the slogan: VIVAT CAROLUS VI. The brass hilt has a shield with an emblem. Owner: Municipal Museum in Karlovy Vary. A similar weapon is owned by the MM.

82

83 An Austrian chevauleger's broadsword from the years 1740 to
1765. It has a straight, two-edged blade, 91 cm long and 4.1 cm
wide. The hilt is of brass and on the guard is the monogram MTJ
(Maria Theresa —Joseph). T.I. 105.5 cm. Owner: MM.

83

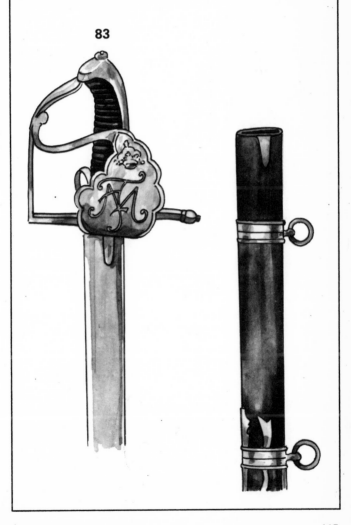

84

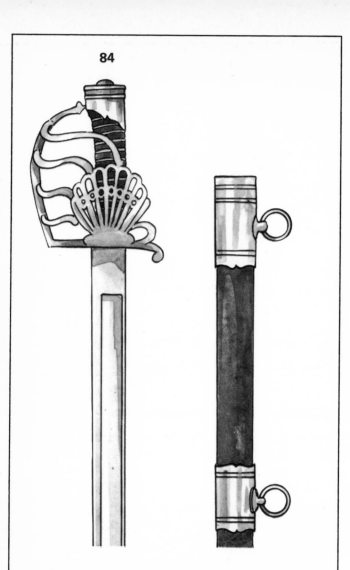

84   A French cavalry officer's sabre from 1788. The same type of sabre with a corresponding hilt, a curved blade and a brass scabbard was used by the officers of the dragoon guards in the years 1806 to 1814. Rousselot, Pl. 14, fig. 12; Pl. 13, fig. 4.

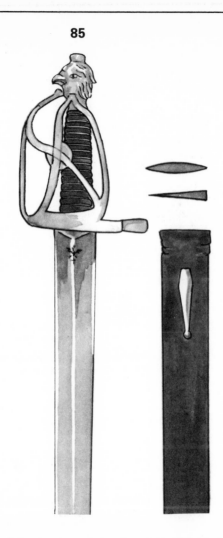

85

85 A Prussian dragoon's broadsword, M. 1732. The blade has the same dimensions as the cuirassier's broadsword and also has the same maker's mark. The grip is covered with leather and ends in a brass eagle's head. The hilt is of brass, with a front and side guard connected by two crossed diagonal bands. Owner: MM.

86 A Russian dragoon's broadsword from the years 1764—1775. The blade is straight and two-edged. The brass hilt has a front guard and three side ones, two of which are crossed. The grip ends in a lion's head. Apart from the last mentioned detail the weapon is identical with the contemporary Prussian broadsword. The scabbard is made of leather and has small brass mounts. Owner: MM.

86

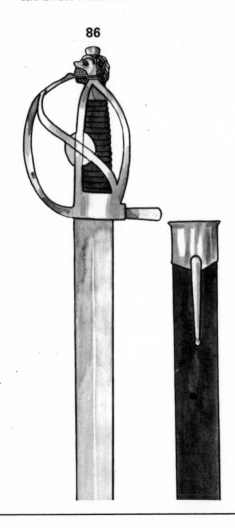

87 A sabre of the French mounted Jaegers' second regiment. M. 1790. The hilt is made of brass in the shape of the letter N. The same weapon was also made with an iron or copper hilt. Rousselot, Pl. 11, fig. 16.

87

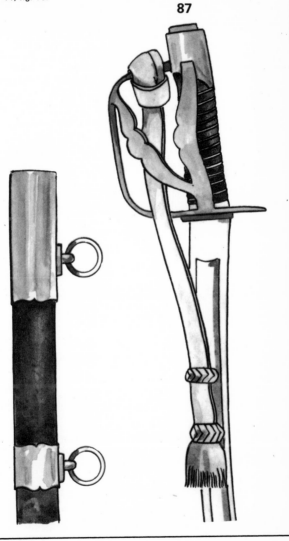

88　A French trooper's broadsword from 1784. The hilt, bearing a *fleur de lys,* and the metal mounts of the scabbard are of copper. Rousselot, Pl. 14, fig. 11.

88

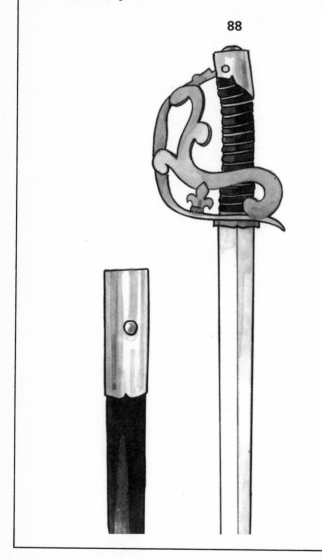

89   A French dragoon's broadsword, M. AN IV, used from 1785 to 1815. Both the hilt and the metal mounts on the scabbard are of steel. The hilt is of the same shape as that of the sabre of 1784, except that in place of the *fleur de lys,* there is a *fasces* and a Jacobin cap. Rousselot, Pl. 7, fig. 19.

89

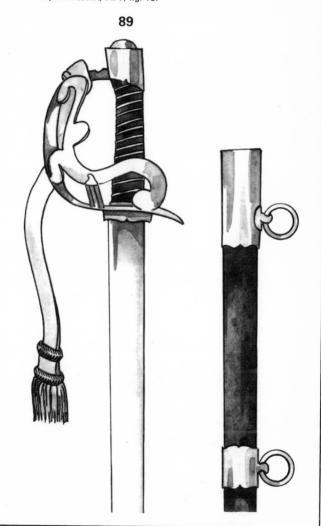

90 A French cuirassier's broadsword, M. AN XI from 1813. The blade
    is straight, single-edged, 95.5 cm long and 3.5 cm wide. On the
    back edge there is engraved: M^{fture} Imp^{le} du Klingenthal Octobre
    1813. The massive hilt is of brass with a wide plate with three
    counter-guards on the outer side. T.l. 111 cm, wt. 1.44 kg. The
    scabbard is of steel. Owner: MM.

90

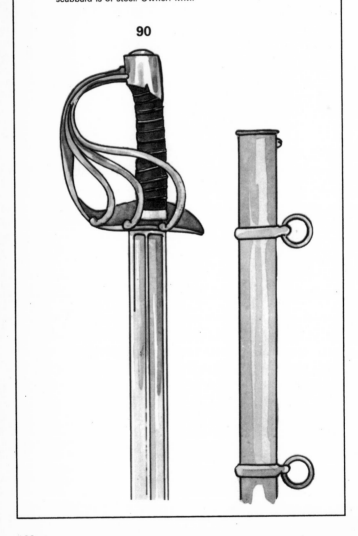

91

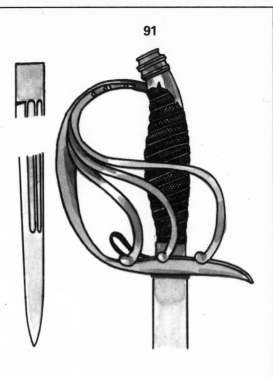

91 A German cuirassier officer's broadsword. The blade is straight, 89 cm long and 2.2 cm broad. The grip is covered with fish-skin. The brass hilt has three counter-guards and between the plate and the grip there is a leather loop for the forefinger. This weapon is known as the 'French' broadsword. T.l. 105 cm. Krickel—Lange, p. 70.

92

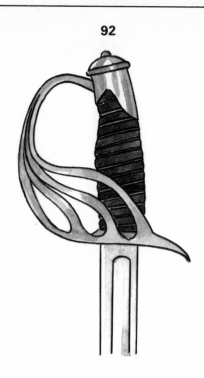

92   A German cuirassier's broadsword, M. 1854, worn by men in all
      German cuirassier regiments from 1876. Both the hilt and the cap
      of the leather grip are made of brass. Krickel —Lange, p. 70.

93 A French heavy cavalry broadsword, M. 1854. The back edge of the straight blade is marked: Mre Imp^ale 'Chât' Janvier 1860 = Carab^er Mle 1854. The massive basket is made of brass and has three counter-guards. Owner: MM.

93

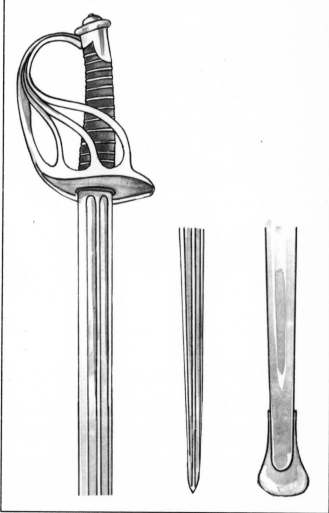

94 A Rumanian officer's sabre of 1907. The blade is slightly curved.
The hilt is swept and decorated and on the guard is the national
emblem. The back rib ends in an eagle's head. The scabbard is
of steel, with two loose hanging rings placed opposite one another.
Owner: MM.

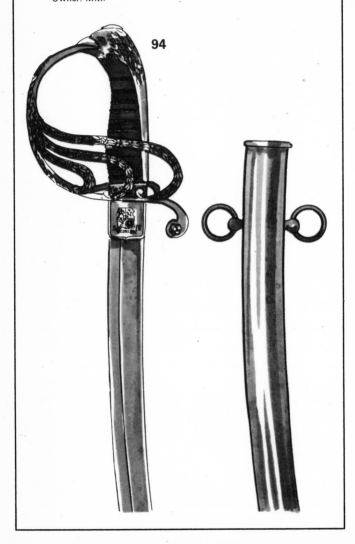

94

95 A Czechoslovak army officer's sabre from between 1925—1939. The blade is slightly curved, 77.6 cm long and 2.5 cm wide. It bears the mark of the maker: Wlaszlovicz —Štós. The hilt is asymmetrical; on the outer side there are wide flat counter-guards ornamented with linden-tree twigs. At the front there is a small emblem of the republic. T.l. 91 cm. The scabbard is of steel. Owner: MM.

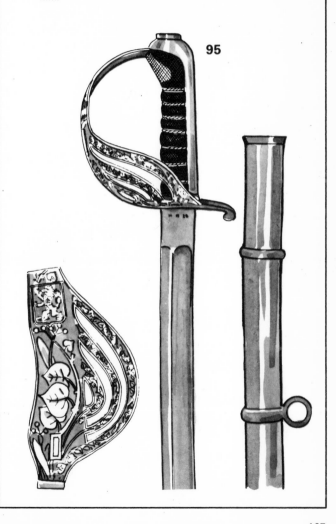

95

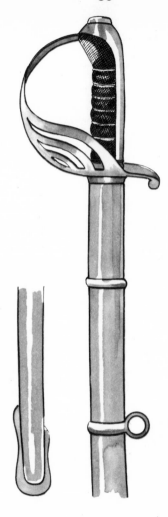

96

96   A Czechoslovak army non-commissioned officer's sabre. It differs from the officer's sabre only in that the hilt is smooth. Owner: MM.

97

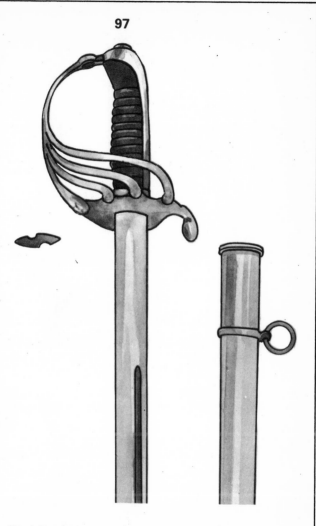

97 A French infantry officer's sword, M. 1882. The blade is straight,
two-edged, with a long thin fuller on each side. L. 85 cm, w.
2.2 cm. On the inner side is engraved the following: Manufacture
Nationale d'Armes de Chatellerault Janvier 1919 Off^{er} d'Infrie
M^{le} 1882. Private collection.

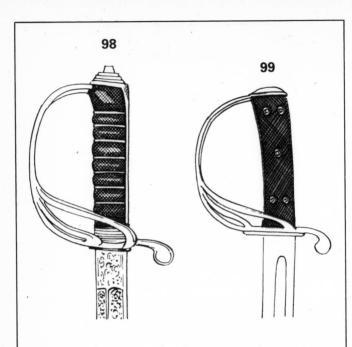

98   An English Royal Artillery and Light Cavalry officer's sword from
     1822. Ffoulkes p. 39, Pl. 34 (H).

99   An English sword for all cavalry troopers, of 1853. Ffoulkes, p. 37,
     Pl. 31 (H).

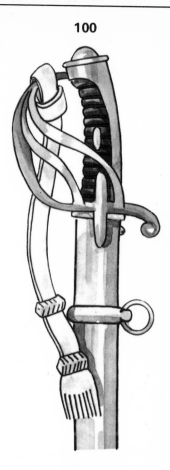

100 A French light cavalry sabre, M. AN XI from the years 1809 —1812. The blade is curved, 87 cm long and 3.5 cm wide. The back edge is marked: M^{fture} Imp^{le} du Klingenthal Mai 1812. The hilt is of brass, with two counter-guards and long langets. T.I. 101.7 cm, wt. 1.25 kg. The scabbard is made of steel. Sabres of this type reached Russia as booty at the time of Napoleon's fall and became part of the Russian army's equipment, but were later manufactured in Russia and bear an inscription in Russian script on the back edge: ZLATOUST 1825 GODA. Owner: NM.

101   A Prussian cavalry sabre of the French type. The blade bears the
      sign: W. K. & C., a royal head and a plumed helmet. The hilt is of
      brass, with two counter-guards, and the back rib ends in an eagle's
      head. From 1858 it was carried by the officers and sergeants of the
      1st Uhlan regiment. Krickel —Lange, p. 50.

101

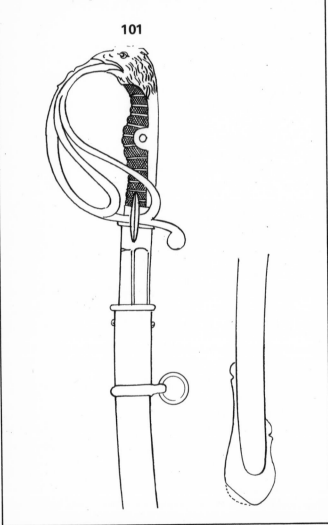

102 A Polish officer's sabre from after the First World War. The blade is curved. The back rib of the grip is of brass and has the Polish eagle marked upon it. The hilt has two counter-guards and wide langets. The scabbard is of steel, with two loose hanging rings. Owner: MM.

102

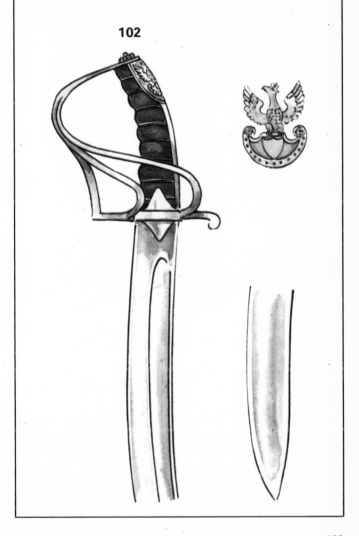

103 A Saxon cavalry guards officer's sword carried until 1918. The
     blade is straight, with a rounded back edge, which develops into
     a rib at the point; it is 88 cm long and 2.7 cm wide. On it is the
     monogram AR and a coronet. The grip is covered with fish-skin,
     the brass back rib ends in a lion's head. The brass hilt has two
     counter-guards. In the centre of the knuckle bow there is the
     Saxon emblem. T.l. 103 cm. Owner: MM.

103

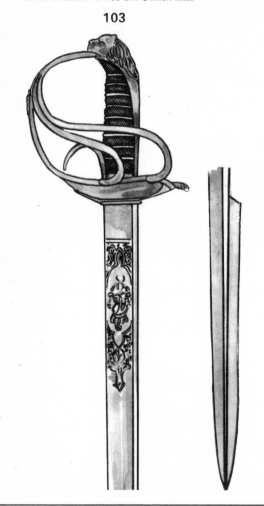

104 A British colonial cavalry troops sabre from 1900. The blade is slightly curved, 92.5 cm long, 3.1 cm wide. The iron hilt has two outer guards and one interrupted inner one. At the top of the knuckle bow there is a slit for the sword knot. T.I. 105.5 cm, wt. 0.98 kg. The whole scabbard including the chape and ferrule is made of leather. Owner: MM.

104

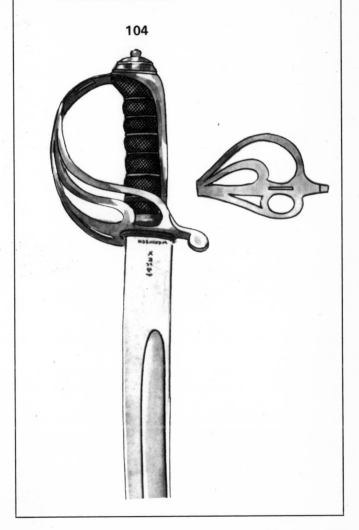

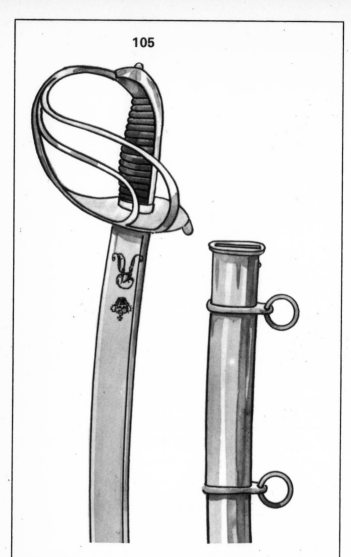

105 A Saxon cavalry sabre, M. 1831. The slightly curved blade is 91 cm long and 3.3 cm wide. It bears the monogram AR and a coronet. On the back edge is engraved: Cv. Keller in Solingen 1831. T.l. 105 cm. Owner: MM.

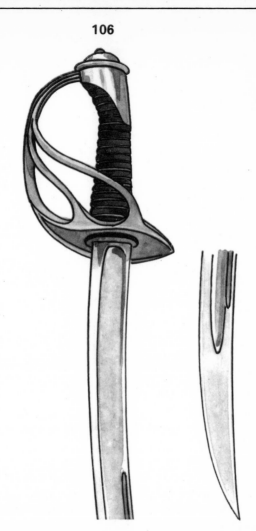

106

106   A French light cavalry sabre, M. 1822 from 1881. The curved blade is 91 cm long, 3 cm wide. On the back edge is the inscription: M^{re} d'Armes de Chât^t Février 1881 Cav^{rie} L^{re} M^{le} 1822. The hilt is of brass, with two counter-guards. The scabbard is of steel. Owner: MM.

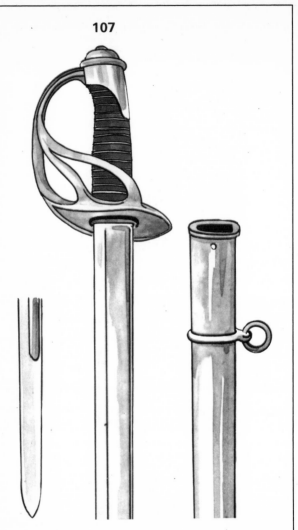

107   A French light cavalry broadsword, M. 1882. The length of the straight blade is 87 cm, the width 2.9 cm. On the back edge are the production details: M^{re} d'Armes de Chât^t Février 1883 = Cav^{rie} Légere M^{le} 1882. The brass hilt has two outer counterguards. The scabbard is of iron. Owner: MM.

108 A German cuirassier broadsword, M. 1819, of the same type as the Russian cuirassier broadsword, which was already in use in Russia by 1808. The weapon has a straight blade and a brass hilt. Conobière: Die blanken Waffen der preussischen Kavallerie. In: AWU Vol. I, p. 123, Pl. 20, figs. 2—3.

108

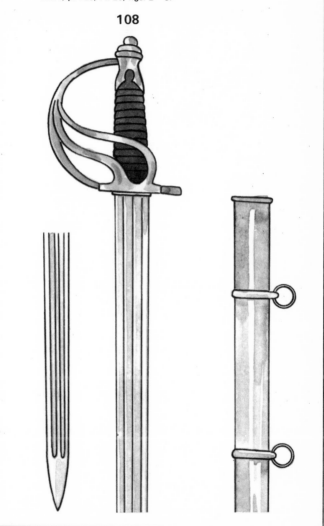

109 A German staff cavalry (Kavallerie-Stabswachen) and field regi-
     ment cuirassier broadsword of the Russian type from the years
     1870—1880. Krickel—Lange p. 70.

110

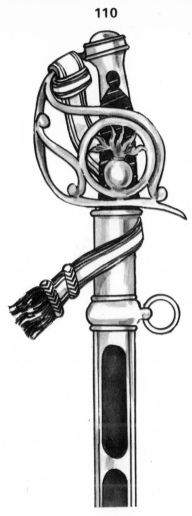

110 A French mounted grenadier's sabre, M. 1806—1814. The blade
is slightly curved. The hilt is of brass with an openwork burning
grenade design between two counter-guards. The scabbard is
entirely of brass, with two pieces cut out, showing the wooden
lining covered with leather. Rousselot, Pl. 13, fig. 11.

111 French royal life guards officer's sabre of 1814. The length of the slightly curved blade is 93 cm, the width 2.9 cm. It bears the Bourbon *fleur de lys* and the inscription: GARDES DU CORPS DU ROI. On the back edge is the sign: Manuf^re R^le de Klingenthal Septembre 1814. The hilt is a swept one, gilded and with the Bourbon escutcheon. Owner: MM.

111

112 A German cavalry broadsword, M. 1889. The blade is straight, developing into a rib at the point. L. 82 cm, w. 2.8 cm. It has the maker's sign: A. F. Hermes Solingen. The grip is of some black material and ends in an iron cap. The openwork iron hilt bears a Prussian eagle in a ring on the outer side. In the upper part of the guard there is a slit for the sword knot. T.l. 97 cm. A broadsword of the same type bears the Württemberg emblem, another the Bavarian emblem. Owner of these weapons: MM.

112

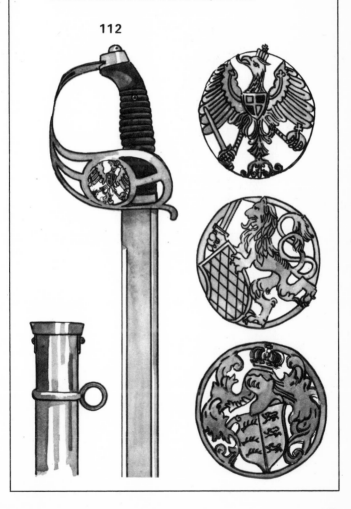

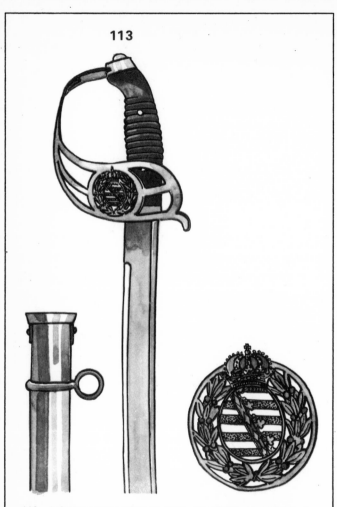

113 A Saxon cavalry sabre, M. 1891. The slightly curved blade has a rounded back edge developing into a rib at the point; l. 78 cm, w. 3.1 cm. The inner side bears the maker's sign: Gebr. Weyserberg Solingen. The openwork iron hilt includes a circular frame with laurel leaves surrounding the Saxony emblem. T.l. 94 cm, wt. 1 kg. Werner Eckhardt—Otto Morawietz: Die Handwaffen des brandenburgisch-preussisch-deutschen Heeres 1640—1945, Hamburg 1957, p. 172. Owner: MM.

114 A Serbian cavalry sabre. The slightly curved blade has a rounded
back edge developing into a rib; l. 88 cm, w. 3 cm. The grip is
bent slightly forward, the top part is ridged and in the lower part
there is a rest for the forefinger. The openwork hilt is assymmetrical
and on the outer side has the Serbian national emblem in an oval.
At the top of the guard there is a slit for the sword knot. T.l. 103 cm.
The scabbard is of steel, with a fixed ring and a stud. Owner: MM.

114

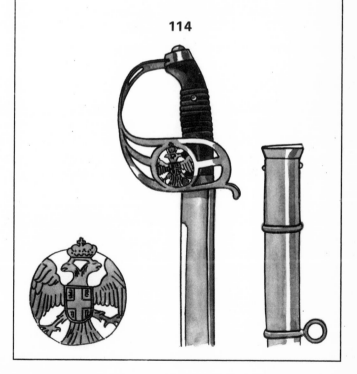

115 A Serbian officer's sabre of 1909. The slightly curved blade is richly ornamented. The grip, made of dark material, ends in a lion's head. The openwork, asymmetrical hilt bears the Serbian emblem within an oval. The maker's sign is: FABRICA DE SOLINGEN 1909. Owner: MM.

115

116

116   A Prussian infantry officer's sword, M. 1889, also carried by officers of the sapper units. The blade is straight, the gilded hilt is ornamented with a crowned eagle and the monogram WR II without a coronet. The monogram WR II with a coronet, made of pressed gilded metal, is fixed to the grip. Krickel — Lange, p. 115, Pl. 315.

117

117   An English infantry officer's sword, M. 1882. The blade is slightly
       curved and on the outer side bears the Star of David. The swept,
       asymmetrical hilt is made of brass and in an oval design bears the
       monogram VR (Queen Victoria 1837—1901) with a distinctive
       rose and thistle. The scabbard is of iron. Owner: MM.

118 A Prussian cavalry sabre, M. 1852. The blade is curved, 86.8 cm long and 3.1 cm wide. The grip is covered with black leather and has an iron back rib. The hilt is of steel, protecting the hand on the outer side with three guards and one on the inner. The maker was Weyersberg & Stamm, Solingen. T.l. 102.5 cm. Krickel—Lange, p. 83, fig. 393.

118

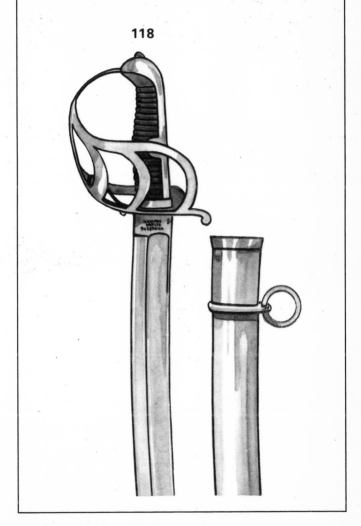

119 An Italian cavalry broadsword. The blade is straight, single-edged. The wooden grip is ridged. The massive iron hilt is asymmetrical. The scabbard is of steel, with a fixed stud and a loose hanging ring. Owner: MM.

119

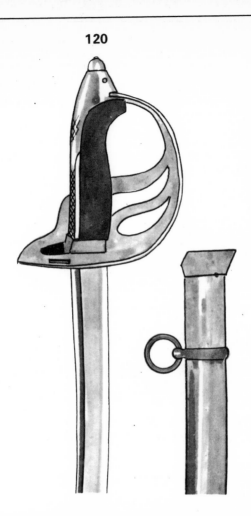

120

120 An Italian cavalry sabre. The blade is slightly curved and has a rounded back edge, developing into a rib at the point; l. 83 cm, w. 2.7 cm. The wooden grip is smooth, with a strong ridged back rib. The massive iron hilt has two guards at the side and an indentation for the thumb. At the back of the inner side of the hilt there is a slit for the sword knot. T.l. 99.5 cm. The scabbard is of steel, with a single loose hanging ring. Owner: MM.

121 A sword for all English cavalry officers from 1834. This type with an openwork hilt was also adopted by the Austrian army for all cavalry officers in 1845. Ffoulkes, p. 37, Pl. 31 (B).

121

122　A sabre for all Austrian cavalry officers from 1845. The curved blade is 88.2 cm long, 3 cm broad. The openwork iron hilt is richly decorated and the pattern is based, it appears, on the English 1834 sword. In the top part of the hilt there is a slit for the sword knot. T.l. 103.5 cm, wt. 0.83 kg. Owner: MM.

122

123

123 An Austrian cavalry officer's sabre of 1850. This weapon is similar to the officer's sabre of 1845, except that it has two slits at the back of the hilt for the sword knot. Adjustierungsvorschrift für die Generäle, Stabs- u. Oberoffiziers der Armee, Wien 1855, Pl. XXIV.

124

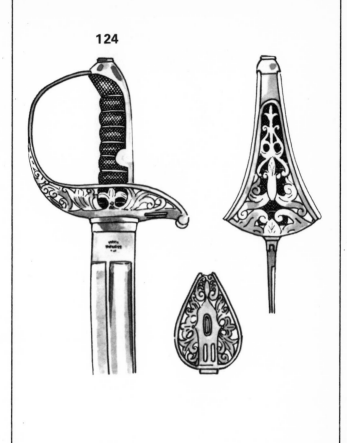

124 An Austrian cavalry officer's sabre, M. 1869. The blade is slightly curved and channelled on the outer side. L. 82.3 cm, w. 3.6 cm. Beneath the hilt is stamped: J. V. GARANTIRT SOLINGEN. The openwork iron hilt has two slits for the sword knot at the back. T.l. 98 cm, w. 0.87 kg. The scabbard is of steel, with a fixed stud at the top and a fixed ring lower down. Owner: MM.

125

125 An Austrian cavalry officer's sabre, M. 1904. The slightly curved blade has a rounded back edge developing into a rib, is 82 cm long and 3 cm wide. The openwork cup hilt is asymmetrical and richly decorated. At the back there are two slits for the sword knots. T.l. 97 cm, wt. 0.88 kg, or 1.43 kg including scabbard. The scabbard is of steel, with an upper lug and lower hanging ring. Owner: MM.

126 An English Life Guard's sword from 1834. Ffoulkes, p. 37, Pl. 31 (A).

127 An English Household Cavalry sword from 1882. Ffoulkes, p. 37, Pl. 31 (B).

128 An English heavy cavalry officer's sabre from 1896. Ffoulkes, p. 37, Pl. 31 (E).

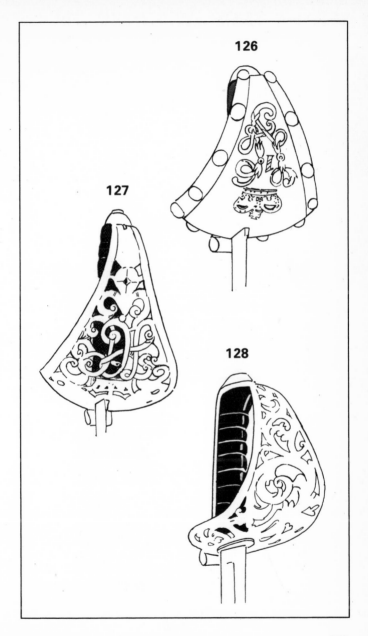

126

127

128

129 An Austrian naval officer's sword, M. 1862. The blade is slightly
curved and the back edge is rounded, developing into a rib at the
point. The Austrian emblem is etched on the outer side of the
blade and a crown and anchor on the inner. The openwork brass
hilt is richly ornamented. In the front, between two Nereids there
is an anchor and a bunch of corals, lower down a two-headed
eagle with the blade passing through its centre. The back rib is
ornamented with the head of Neptune, beneath which there is his
trident. The scabbard is covered with leather and has brass mounts.
The upper part is ornamented with an anchor. Owner: MM.

129

130

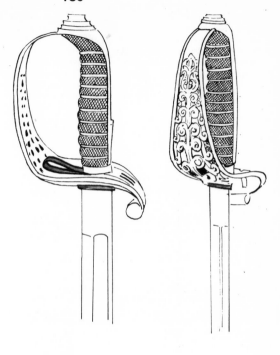

130   A sabre carried by the Hesse officers of the 115th—118th infantry regiments of the Grand Duke of Hesse. It has a curved blade and the openwork hilt and the back rib of the grip are gilded. Krickel—Lange, p. 44.

131

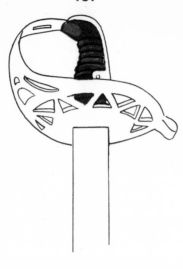

131 An English cavalry sabre from the beginning of the 19th century. The hilt has a slit for the sword knot in the upper part of the knuckle bow. Ffoulkes, p. 38, Pl. 34 (C).

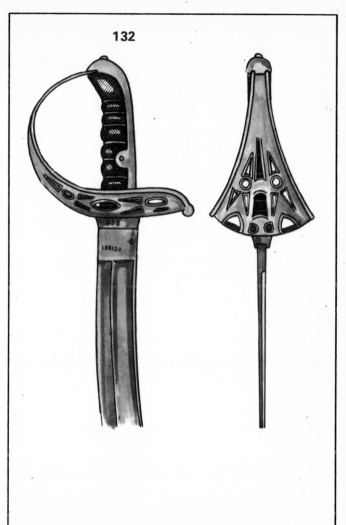

132

132 An Austrian cavalry sabre, M. 1861. The blade is slightly curved, 84 cm long, 3.3 cm wide and with a fuller only on the outer side, the inner side being smooth. The iron hilt has circular and triangular perforations. T.l. 100 cm. The scabbard is of steel, with a fixed stud on the inner side at the top and a fixed ring lower down. Owner: MM.

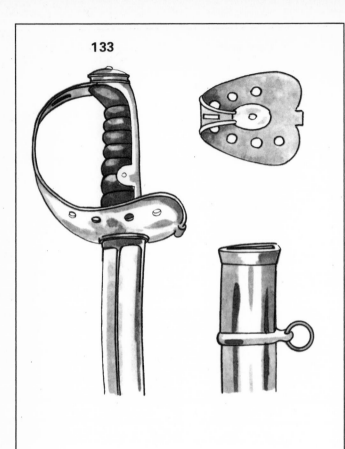

133 An Austrian cavalry sabre, M. 1845. The blade is curved. The hilt
is of steel, pierced with seven small circular holes. At the top of the
hilt there is a slit for the sword knot. The scabbard is of iron, with
two loose hanging rings. These sabres were intended for all cavalry. Owner: MM.

134 An English cavalry sabre of 1830. The shell guard has a slit for the
     sword knot at the top. Ffoulkes, p. 36, Pl. 31 (G).

134

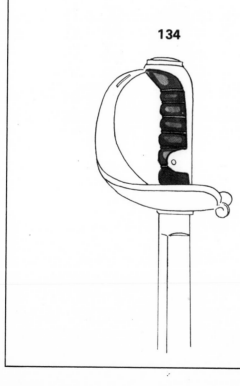

135 An Austrian cavalry sabre, M. 1850. The blade is curved. The guard is of steel, with circular perforations and at the back it has two slits for the sword knot. The scabbard is of iron, with two loose hanging rings. Owner: MM.

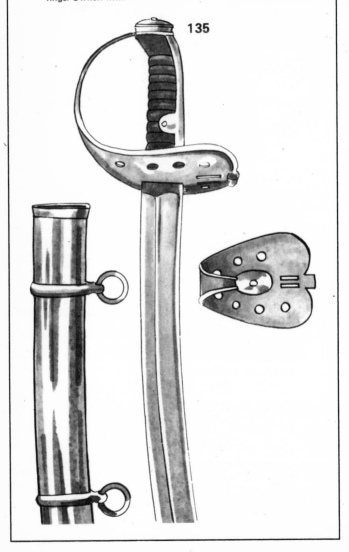

135

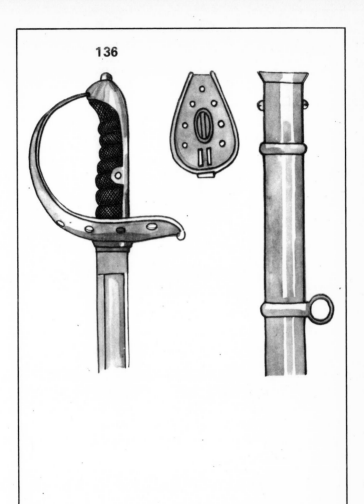

136

136   An Austrian cavalry sabre, M. 1869. The slightly curved blade is 84 cm long, 3.6 cm wide and fullered only on one side. The hilt is of steel, with seven circular perforations. T.l. 100 cm, wt. 1.20 kg. The scabbard is of iron, with a fixed stud and a fixed ring for suspension at the belt. Adjustierungs- u. Ausrüstungsvorschrift für das k.k. Heer, Wien 1878, p. 185. Owner: NM.

137 An Austrian cavalry sabre, M. 1904. The blade is slightly curved with a rounded back edge that develops into a rib. The steel hilt is somewhat wider on the outer side. In order to lighten the weight it is perforated with twenty-seven circular holes. T.l. 103 cm, wt. 1.04 kg, or 1.74 kg with scabbard. The scabbard is of steel with a fixed lug and a fixed ring lower down. Owner: MM.

137

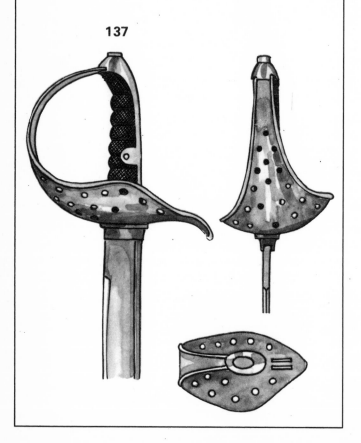

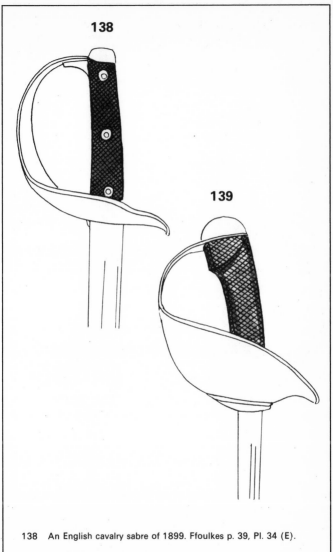

138 An English cavalry sabre of 1899. Ffoulkes p. 39, Pl. 34 (E).

139 An English cavalry broadsword of 1908 with a shell guard and a hatched grip with an iron cap. Ffoulkes p. 39, Pl. 34 (F). Owner: Municipal Museum in Kostelec nad Černými lesy (Bohemia).

140 A Spanish mounted jaeger's broadsword. It is a weapon of honour,
     presented to Francis Ferdinand d'Este as the honorary colonel of
     the 12th regiment. It bears the inscription: FABRICA DE TOLEDO
     and a dedication: A SU CORONEL HONORARIO S.A.T.Y.R.
     ARCHIDUQUE FRANCISCO FERNANDO LOS JEFES Y OFICIA-
     LES DE CAZADORES D'LUSITANIA 12° DE CABALERIA. Owner:
     MM.

140

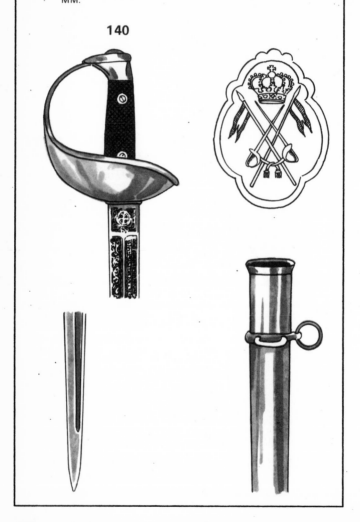

141 An Austrian heavy cavalry broadsword, M. 1769/75, with a straight single-edged blade which is 81 cm long and 3.5 cm wide. Engraved upon it is the Austrian eagle. The steel hilt is simple, broad, with two langets. T.l. 97.3 cm, wt. 0.90 kg or 2.10 kg with the scabbard. In 1775 the wooden leather-covered scabbard was replaced with an iron one. Owner: MM.

141

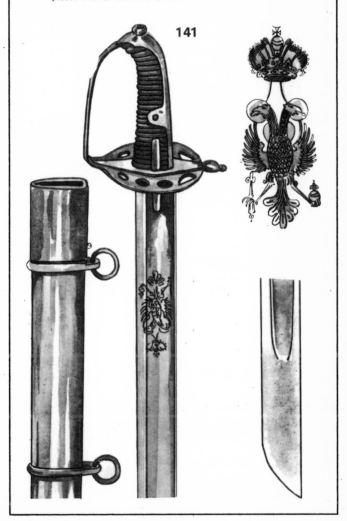

142 An English cavalry broadsword of 1807. This weapon is very similar to the broadsword for the Austrian cavalry, issued to the
cuirassiers, dragoons, and chevaulegers in 1769. Ffoulkes, p. 39,
Pl. 34 (D).

143 An Austrian heavy cavalry, non-commissioned officer's broadsword, M. 1769. The single-edged blade is straight, 83 cm long,
3.5 cm wide. The two-headed Austrian eagle with a coronet is engraved on both sides of the blade, and on the back edge is the
place of production: Pottenstein. The hilt is of brass and the back
rib of the grip ends in a lion's head. T.l. 97.5 cm, wt. 0.90 kg.
Owner: MM.

143

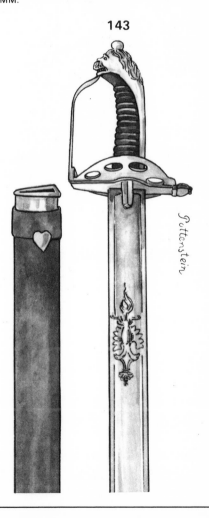

144 An Austrian heavy cavalry broadsword, M. 1803. It has a straight
blade, l. 84.5 cm, w. 3.5 cm. The hilt is a simple iron one with eight
circular perforations. At the back are two slits for the sword knot.
Teuber—Ottenfeld, Pl. Blanke Waffen der Kavallerie, fig. 5.

144

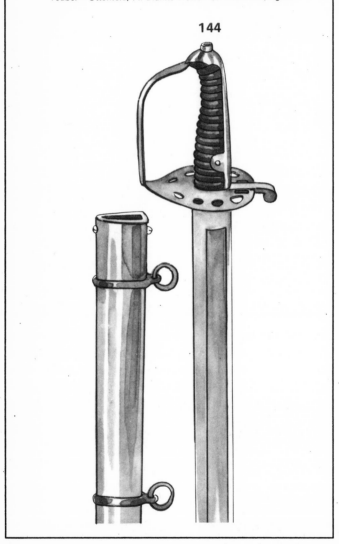

145 An Austrian heavy cavalry non-commissioned officer's broadsword of 1798. The straight blade bears the monogram F II and a coronet (Franz II as Holy Roman emperor and Franz I as Austrian emperor; 1768—1835). The simple hilt is made of iron. The scabbard is also of iron. Owner: MM.

145

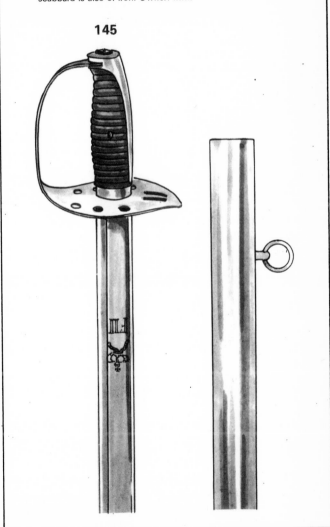

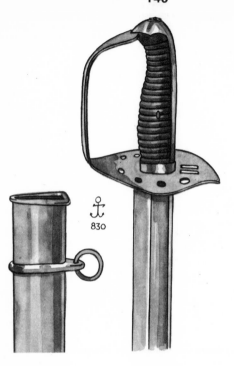

830

146 An Austrian heavy cavalry broadsword from around 1824. The blade is straight, 85 cm long and 3.3 cm broad. The name of the maker, Fischer, is stamped on it together with an anchor. On the lower part of the steel hilt there are seven holes and two slits for the sword knot. T.l. 101 cm, wt. 1.05 kg. Owner: MM.

147 An Austrian heavy cavalry broadsword from around 1800. The single-edged blade is straight, length 86.3 cm, width 3.3 cm. It bears the monogram F II with a coronet on either side. The name of the maker, Fischer, is stamped on the back edge. The steel hilt has a single guard for the protection of the outer side of the hand. Owner: MM.

147

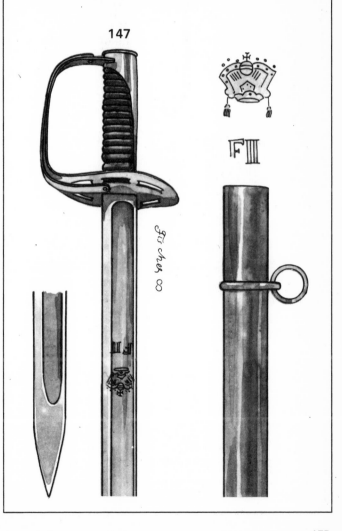

148 An Austrian hussar staff officer's sabre, M. 1827. The length of the curved blade is 84.5 cm, the width 3.9 cm. The steel hilt has a single guard. At the back there are two slits for the sword knot. Owner: MM.

148

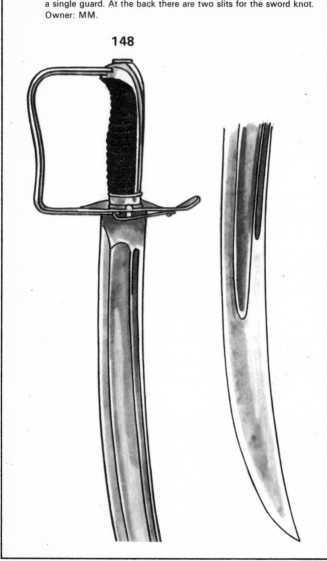

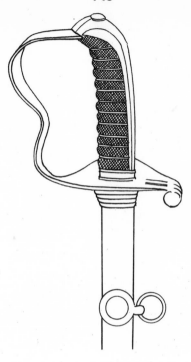

149   A Baden officer's sabre carried by the officers of the 109th and
       110th Baden grenadier regiments and by the 111th—114th in-
       fantry regiments. The blade is slightly curved. Part of the hilt and
       the scabbard are made of steel plate. Krickel — Lange, p. 38.

150 An Austrian infantry officer's sabre, M. 1861. The blade is slightly curved, grooved on both sides; l. 79.5 cm, w. 2.4 cm. The simple hilt is of steel, with two slits for the sword knot at the back. T.l. 93.5 cm. The scabbard is of iron, with one fixed stud and one fixed ring. Owner: MM.

150

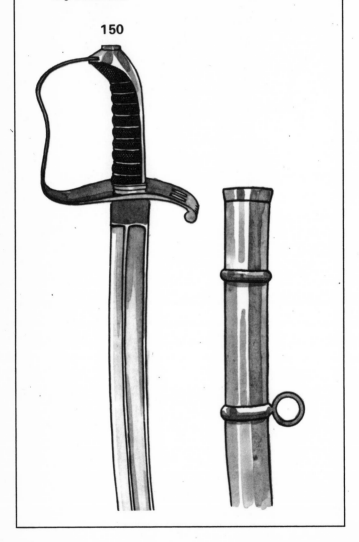

151

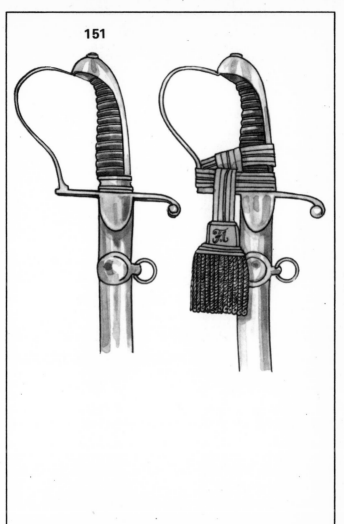

151　An Austrian officer's sabre, M. 1837. The blade is curved, with grooves on both sides; l. 84 cm, w. 2.5 cm. The knuckle bow is narrow and widens at the top. The cross-guard has two broad semi-circular langets. T.l. 97.5 cm. The scabbard is of steel, with two loose hanging rings. Zur Adjustierungsvorschrift vom Jahre 1837 (Österreich) Pl. 4.

152

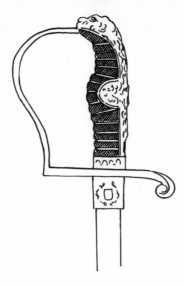

152   A Prussian officer's sabre, M. 1889. It was carried by the sergeants and standard bearers who had passed the officer's test of the Prussian 3rd—5th dragoon regiments. Krickel—Lange, p. 83, Pl. 394.

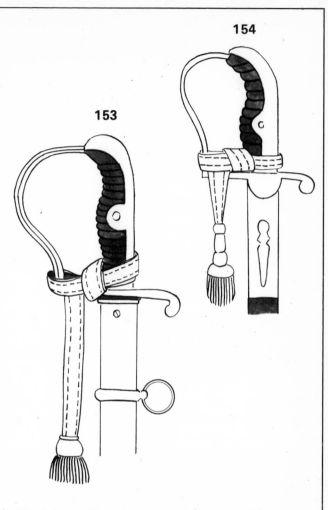

153

154

153　A German Uhlan sabre, M. 1873, carried by the men of the 1st to 8th Uhlan regiments. Krickel—Lange, p. 107.

154　A Prussian fusilier's sword. It was carried by the officers and sergeant majors of the fusilier battalions of the infantry guards regiments, the fusilier guards regiment and the jaeger and riflemen battalions. Krickel—Lange, p. 14.

155

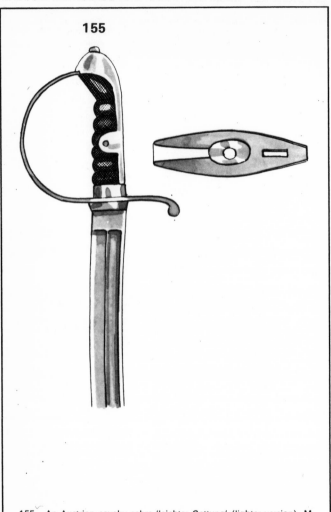

155   An Austrian cavalry sabre 'leichter Gattung' (lighter version), M.
      1877. The blade is slightly curved, with deep grooves on both
      sides; l. 77 cm, w. 3.1 cm. It bears the name of the maker JOH.
      ZELINKA WIEN. The hilt is narrow, with a slit for the sword knot
      at the back. The steel scabbard has a fixed stud both on the outer
      and on the inner sides near the top and a fixed ring lower down.
      Owner: MM.

156 An Austrian cuirassier broadsword from the beginning of the 18th century. The two-edged blade is straight, 92 cm long. The Austrian eagle and coronet with the following inscription is engraved on both sides: VIVAT ERTZ-HERTZOG JOSEPH (Joseph I, 1678 to 1711, ascended the throne on 5 May 1705). The hilt consists of a simple brass knuckle bow with langet and a thumb ring. Owner: MM.

156

157 An Austrian hussar's estoc from around 1700. The blade is straight, 100—150 cm long. The weapon was placed on the right side along the flank of the horse, beneath the saddle and stirrups. Quirin Leitner: Die Waffensammlung des österreichischen Kaiserhauses im k.k. Artillerie-Arsenal-Museum in Wien, Vienna, 1866—1870, Pl. XLIV.

157

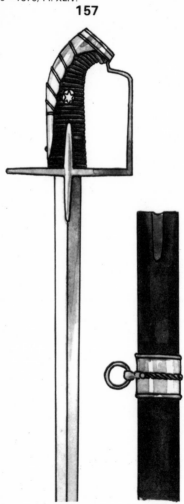

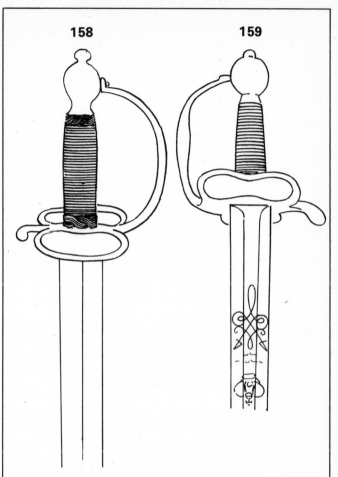

158   A Russian dragoon's broadsword from around 1700. The blade is straight, the hilt consists of a two-winged symmetrical shell and a simple knuckle guard. A. V. Viskovatov: Istoricheskoye opisaniye odiezhdy i vooruzheniya rossiyskikh voysk, St Petersburg, 1899, II, Pl. 188—190.

159   A Danish sword, M. 1705. The straight two-edged blade is 71.5 cm long and 3.3 cm wide. The whole weapon is 87.4 cm long. Vaabenhistoriske Aarbøger IX a—c, Copenhagen, 1957, p. 124—125.

160 A .French cavalry broadsword from 1750. The straight blade is
89.5 cm long. The copper hilt has a heart-shaped shell and two
counter-guards. The scabbard is wooden, covered with leather,
and has copper mounts. Owner: MM.

160

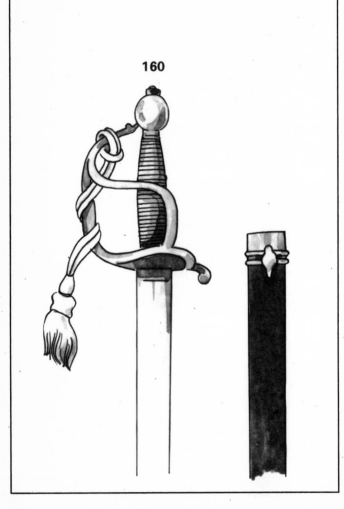

161 A French cavalry sabre of 1824. The blade is curved, the brass hilt
   has a bordering guard plate, from which the knuckle bow projects. Owner: MM.

161

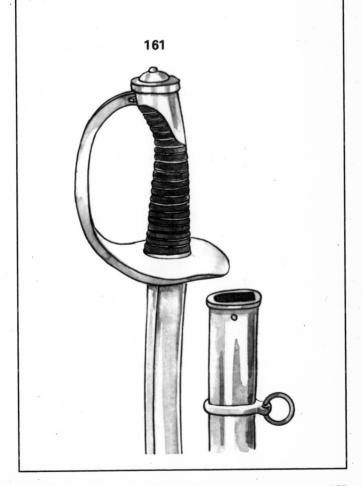

162 A Polish cavalry sabre of 1791. The curved blade is 82.7 cm long, 3.5 cm wide. There is an inscription: KONSTITUCIA and the monogram SAR with a coronet, beneath which there is another inscription: 3 MAJA RUKA 1791. On the inner side in the middle of the slogan: NAROD Z KRÓLEM, KRÓL Z NARODEM, there is engraved a figure of an uhlan. T.l. 95.5 cm, wt. 0.90 kg. The brass hilt is pierced. Owner: MM.

162

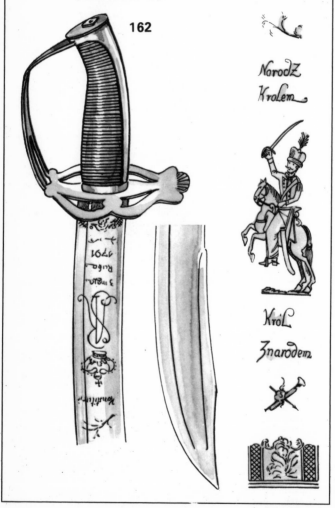

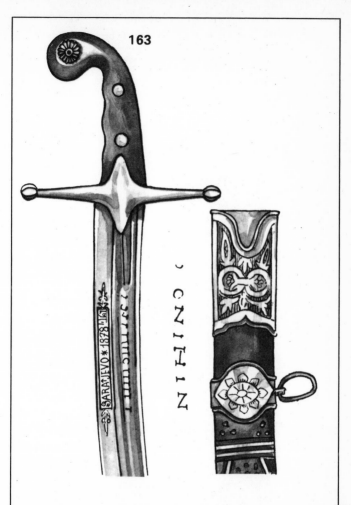

163 An Oriental type Yugoslav sabre from 1878. The length of the curved blade is 79 cm, the width 3.2 cm. It is fullered and bears the inscription: SARAJEVO 1878 on a silver plate and on another one: NIHINO or ONIHIN, depending on whether it is read from left to right or vice versa. The grip is of horn, curving forwards at the top, with a hole for the sword knot. The quillons are of brass and have langets. The scabbard is covered with leather and has brass mounts. Private collection.

164 An Austrian hussar sabre from around 1700. The curved blade was usually 72—84 cm long. The scabbard has perforated brass mounts, underlaid with red cloth. (These weapons were made by Gypsies). Teuber—Ottenfeld, Pl. Blanke Waffen der Kavallerie, fig. 8.

164

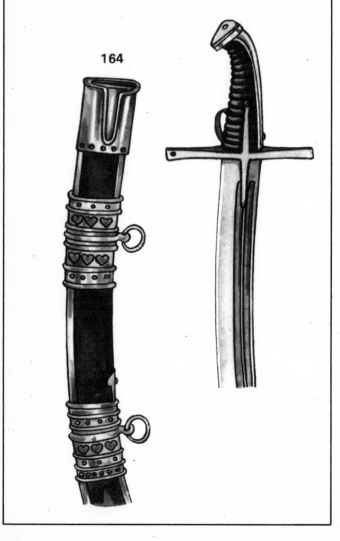

165 An Austrian hussar sabre from the end of the 17th century. The
blade is slightly curved. The quillons turn upwards at right angles
at the front and have long langets. Owner: Municipal Museum in
Karlovy Vary.

165

166

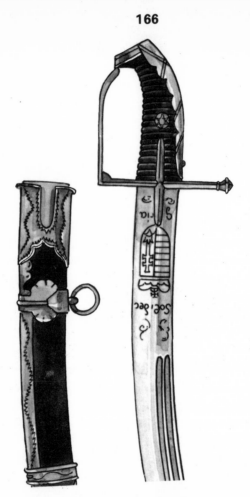

166 An Austrian hussar's sabre dated 1744 and meant perhaps for
officers or sergeants. The length of the curved blade is 92 cm. On
the outer side is the Hungarian emblem and the inscription: SOLI
DEO GLORIA, on the inner side there is a figure of a hussar and
the slogan: VINCERE AUT MORI. On the back edge is engraved:
W. Neustadt anno 1744. The scabbard has decorated brass
mounts. Owner: MM.

167 A sabre carried by officers of the Austrian hussar regiment of Prince Paul Eszterhazy from 1741 to 1775. It is interesting to note the ornamentation of the knuckle bow, which represents a string of pearls. Anton Dolleczek: Monographie der k. u k. österreichisch-ungarischen blanken u. Handfeuer-Waffen, Vienna, 1896, Pl. II.

167

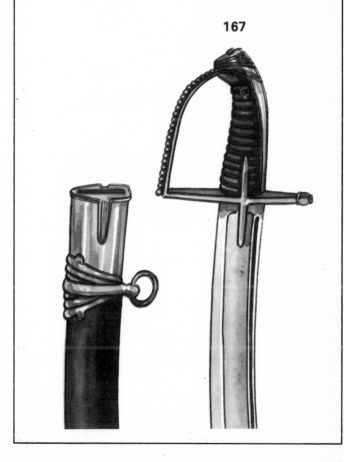

168

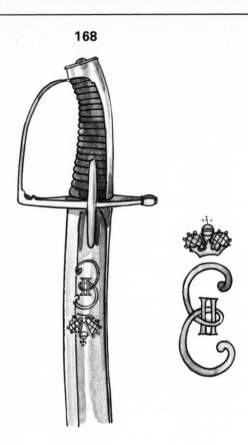

168 A Russian hussar's sabre from the years 1762—1796. The blade
is curved and hollowed out on both sides. On the outer side is engraved the monogram of Catherine II: E II (Ekaterina) with a coronet. The narrow brass hilt has long langets. Owner: MM.

169 A French mounted jaeger guard's sabre, M. 1802. The blade is curved, 87.5 cm long, 3.4 cm wide. On the back edge are the manufacturer's marks: M^{fture} Imp^{le} du Klingenthal août 1813. The brass hilt is narrow, with langets. T.l. 102 cm. The brass scabbard has a wooden lining. In the upper half there is a long cut-out, under-padded with leather. Owner: MM.

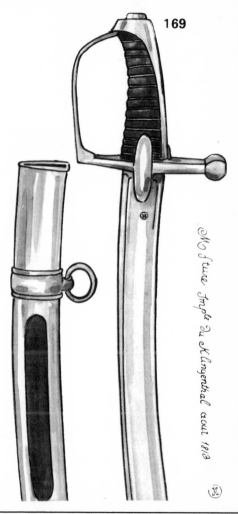

169

170

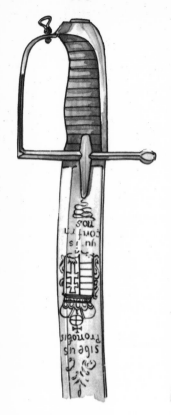

170 An Austrian pandour sabre, perhaps that of an officer and dating from 1747. The length of the curved blade is 74.5 cm, the width 3.3 cm. On the outer side there is the Hungarian emblem in the middle of the slogan: SIBEUS (Si Deus) PRO NOBIS, QUIS CONTRA NOS. On the inner side there is a pandour soldier and the inscription: PUGNO PRO PATRIA. On the back edge there is engraved: Mairschoffer in Passau anno 1747. T.l. 87 cm, wt. 0.78 kg. Owner: MM.

171 A Prussian hussar sabre from the middle of the 18th century. The curved blade has a single narrow fuller on each side; l. 80 cm, w. 3.7 cm. On the blade is stamped: POTZDAM and a small Prussian eagle. The grip, covered with leather, has a steel back rib. The hilt is narrow, with long langets. T.l. 103 cm, wt. 0.90 kg. The wooden scabbard is covered with leather and has large steel mounts. Sammlung Hollitzer, Pl. XXVIII, No. 276. Owner: MM.

171

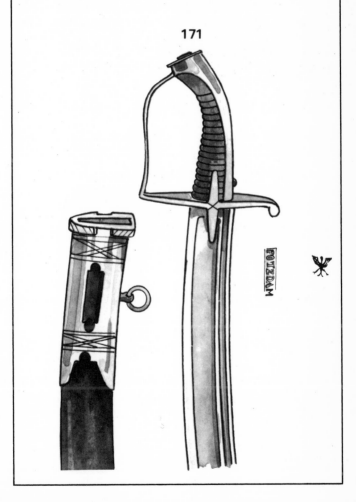

172 An Austrian hussar sergeant's sabre, M. 1768. In size this sabre corresponds to that of the regular soldier. The blade is curved, 85 cm long, 3.9 cm wide, with an Austrian eagle stamped on it. Both the hilt and the metal mounts of the scabbard are of brass. T.l. 97 cm, wt. 0.90 kg. Allgemeiner Aufriß und Beschreibungen Sammentlicher Montours- und Rüstungs-Gattungen, Feld-Requisiten und Kriegs-Gerätschaften für die Kais.-Königl. Truppen zu Fuß und zu Pferd, a manuscript from the years 1769—1775, Vol. III, Pl. 39—40 (Prague, Military Museum, registration mark G 22).

172

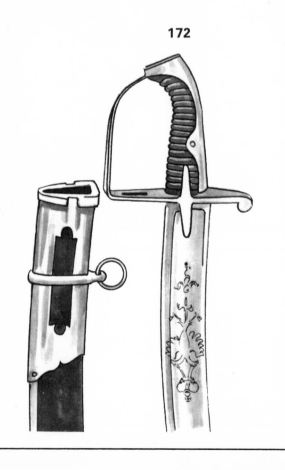

173

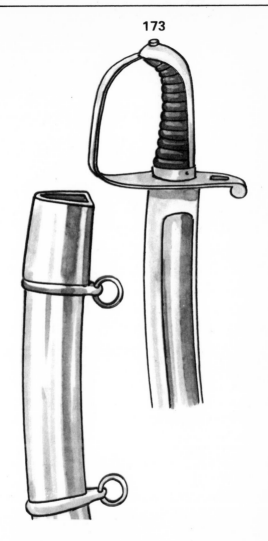

173 An Austrian hussar's sabre, M. 1803. The blade is curved, 83 cm long and 3.5 cm wide. The iron hilt is narrow, with a slit for the sword knot at the back. T.l. 97 cm, wt. 0.90 kg. The scabbard is also of iron. Owner: MM.

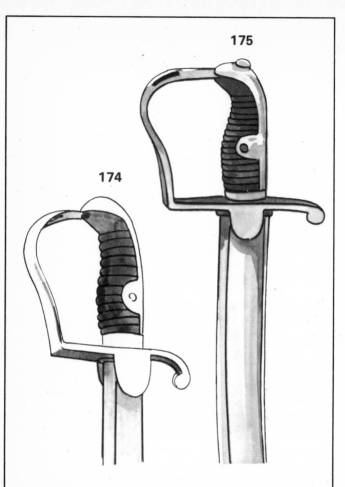

175

174

174 An English light cavalry trooper's sabre from 1796. In Prussia this type of sabre was introduced as the cavalry sabre in 1811. Ffoulkes p. 39, Pl. 34 (G).

175 A Prussian cavalry sabre, M. 1811. It was carried by the dragoons, hussars and the mounted train units. The blade is slightly curved. The narrow hilt widens slightly and has a slit for the sword knot at the top. The scabbard is of steel. Werner Eckhardt —Otto Mora-wietz: Die Handwaffen des branderburgisch-preussisch-deut-schen Heeres 1640 —1945, Hamburg 1957, p. 72.

176 A Hungarian infantry officer's sabre, M. 1811, type I (Austria).
After 1827 this was also carried by the grenadier and jaeger officers. The curved blade is 77—84 cm long. The narrow brass hilt
has small langets. Anton Dolleczek: Monographie der k. u. k. österreichisch-ungarischen blanken u. Handfeuer-Waffen, Vienna,
1896, pp. 27—28.

176

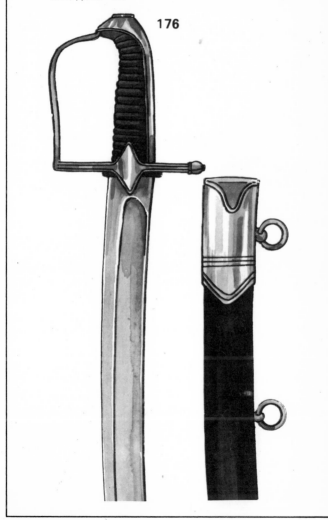

177 A Hungarian infantry officer's sabre, M. 1811, type II. The curved blade is 85 cm long, 2.7 cm wide. The narrow brass hilt has langets decorated with rosettes and rays. T.l. 98.5 cm, wt. 0.74 kg. Owner: MM.

178 A Polish cavalry sabre from the beginning of the 19th century. The blade is slightly curved, the narrow angular hilt has semi-circular langets and a ridged wooden grip. Księga jazdy Polskiej p. 113. Owner: MM.

177   **178**

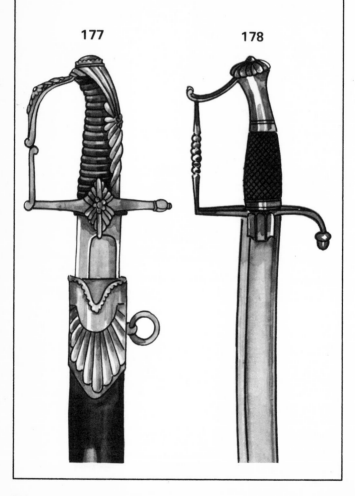

179 A Polish cavalry sabre from the second quarter of the 20th century. The length of the slightly curved blade is 82.3 cm, the width 3.3 cm. There is a diagonally ridged wooden grip secured by two screws and a brass cap. The narrow hilt is of brass, with two langets and a horizontal loop for the sword knot. T.l. 96 cm. The scabbard is of steel, with one stud and a suspension ring. Owner: MM.

179

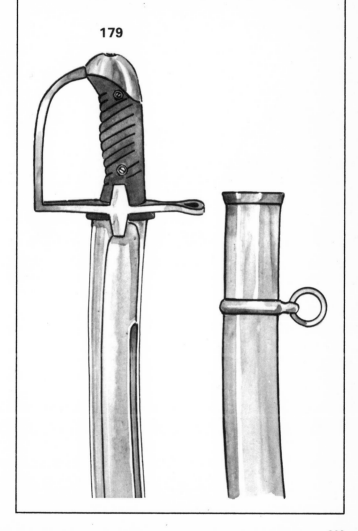

180 A French mounted artillery sabre, M. 1829 dating from 1851. The length of the curved blade is 81 cm, the width 2.9 cm. It bears the inscription: Manu^fre N^le Châtellerault Janvier 1851. The hilt is narrow and the guard is made of brass. T.l. 98.1 cm, wt. 1.92 kg. Owner: MM.

180

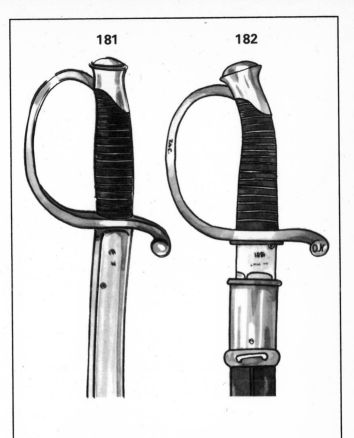

181 **182**

181   A Russian dragoon's sabre from 1854. The blade is slightly curved,
with fullers on both sides; l. 87.5 cm, w. 3.5 cm. On the back edge
there is an inscription in Russian script: ZLATOUST 1854. The
grip is covered with leather. The hilt is of brass. T.l. 101 cm, wt.
1.03 kg. The scabbard is of wood, covered with leather and has
brass mounts. Owner: MM.

182   A Russian trooper's sabre from 1881. The blade is slightly curved,
grooved on both sides, with the date 1881 stamped on the outer
side; l. 74.2 cm, w. 3 cm. The grip is covered with leather and
bound with brass wire. The hilt is of brass. The wooden scabbard
is covered with leather and has brass mounts and there is a fixed
stud and a loose triangular loop lower down on the blade-edge
side. Owner: MM.

183 A Russian officer's sabre from the beginning of the 20th century. The blade is slightly curved, hollowed on both sides, with two unequal grooves; l. 79 cm, w. 3.2 cm. Some weapons of this type have an etched and engraved imperial eagle on the outer side of the blade and the ruler's monogram N II on the inner. The grip is dark, horizontally ridged and has a brass cap ornamented with a laurel twig. The brass hilt is decorated with a simple stripe design. T.l. 93.5 cm. The scabbard is wooden, covered with leather and has brass mounts. Owner: MM.

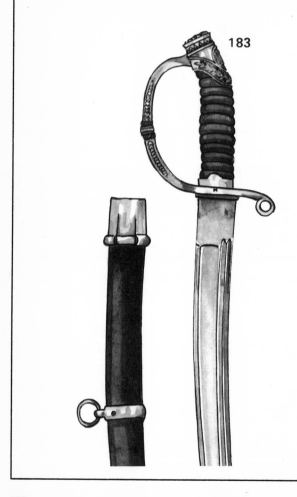

183

184 A Russian dragoon's sabre from 1908—1909. The blade is slightly curved. The grip is wooden and diagonally ridged. The hilt is made of brass, with a circular hole for the sword knot at the back. The scabbard is of wood, covered with leather and then lacquered. The metal mounts, including the fixtures for a bayonet, are of brass. Owner: MM.

184

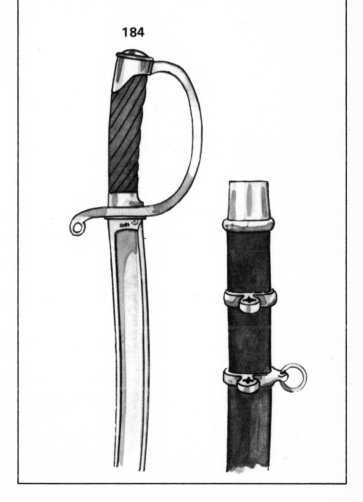

185   The Cossack *shashka* from 1910. The blade is slightly curved,
      74.5 cm long, 3.5 cm wide. On the outer side is an ornament which
      bears an inscription in Russian script: ZOF 1910 G. The grip has
      a black haft, ending at the top in a typical pommel. T.l. 90.5 cm,
      wt. 0.73 kg. The wooden scabbard is covered with leather and has
      silver mounts. The mouth of the scabbard of a *shashka* was so
      shaped that the weapon could be sheathed right up to the pommel.
      This type of weapon originated in the Caucasus. Owner: MM.

185

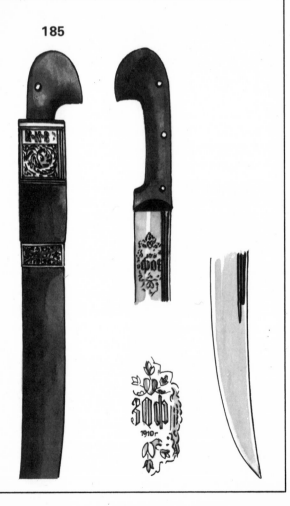

186 A Cossack sabre of 1851. The length of the curved blade is
84.5 cm, the width 3.3 cm. On the back edge is engraved in
Russian script: ZLATOUST IYUNYA 1851 GODA. The grip,
which is covered with leather, has a brass back rib that curves up
at the front in the shape of a beak. At the top there is a circular
hole for the sword knot. T.I. 98.5 cm. The scabbard is of wood,
covered with leather, and has brass mounts. Owner: MM.

187 The Don Cossack type sabre from 1918. The blade is slightly
curved and on the inner side has the date 1918 and formed in
a circle the inscription in Russian script: ZLATOUST OR. FABR.
The wooden grip is diagonally ridged. The brass pommel is cut out
at the top and has a circular hole in the centre for the sword knot.
The scabbard is of wood, covered with leather and lacquered
black. Those sabres, which were taken over by the Red Army or
actually produced under the Soviet government, bear the Soviet
emblem or a five-pointed star. Owner: MM.

186 **187**

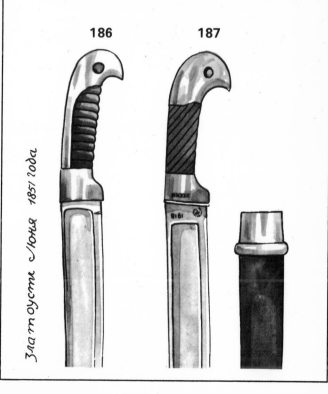

Златоустъ Іюня 1851 года

188

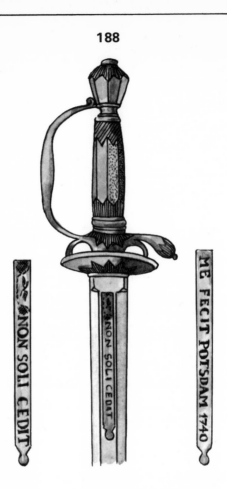

188 A Prussian officer's sword from 1740. The blade is straight and two-edged. There are brass plaques inlaid on both sides. On the outer side is engraved: NON SOLI CEDIT and on the inner: ME FECIT POTSDAM 1740. The grip is cast from brass as is the shell. Owner: MM.

189 A Prussian officer's sword from the middle of the 18th century.
The straight blade is 2.5 cm wide and decorated on both sides. On
the outer side there is the monogram FR with a coronet. The hilt is
of brass, the grip is wound with copper wire. Owner: MM.

189

190 An Austrian officer's sword from the first half of the 18th century.
The two-edged blade is straight, 86.4 cm long and 2.5 cm wide.
On either side is engraved the number 1417 and the Passau wolf
sign. The brass hilt is richly ornamented. T.I. 104 cm. Owner: NM.

190

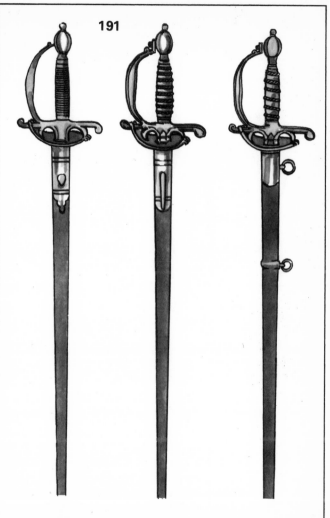

191 Types of Austrian officers' swords:
a) 1740
b) 1798
c) 1811
The length of the blades vary between 75 and 85 cm. Teuber—
Ottenfeld, p. 828.

192 An Austrian officer's sword from 1827. The blade is 83.5 cm long and 2.4 cm wide. Total length of the weapon is 105 cm, weight 0.81 kg. The brass hilt is gilded. Adjustierungsvorschrift für das k. u. k. Heer vom Jahre 1827, p. 9, Pl. I. Owner: MM.

192

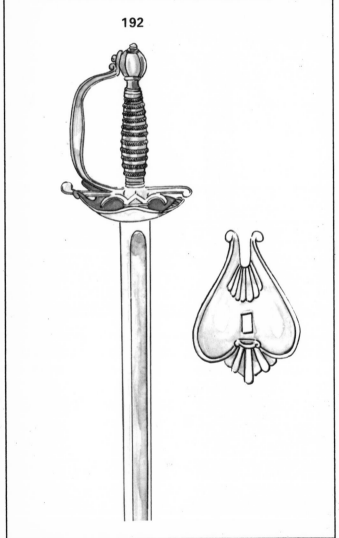

193 A Saxon officer's sword of the 18th century. It has a straight two-edged blade, upon which are the initials AR and a coronet; l. 82.2 cm, w. 2.3 cm. The hilt is of brass and the grip is wound with copper wire. Private collection.

193

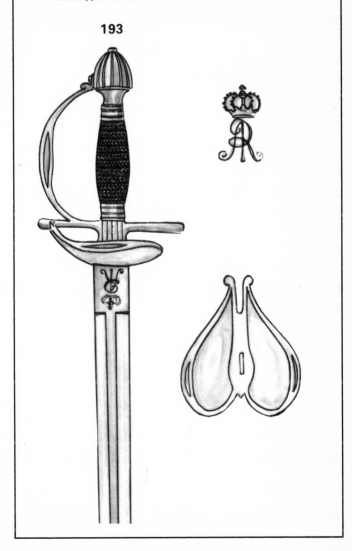

194 **195**

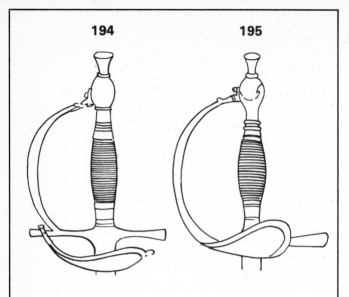

194   A Prussian sword of the Russian type, carried by the cuirassier officers. Krickel — Lange, p. 71, fig. 18.

195   A Prussian sword of the French type and carried until 1876 by the cuirassier officers when off duty (ausser Dienst). Krickel — Lange, p. 71, fig. 17.

196 An Austrian officer's sword, M. 1837. The blade is 80 cm long and 2.3 cm wide. The hilt is of brass. T.l. 94 cm. Owner: MM.

197 A Prussian sword. Carried by the officers and sergeant-majors of the 1st and 2nd battalions of the 1st—4th infantry guards regiments. Krickel—Lange, p. 14.

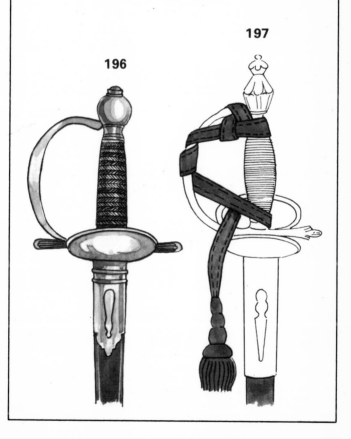

196

197

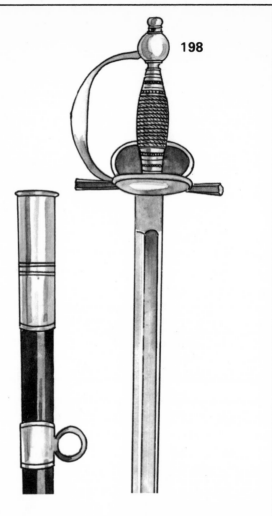

198　A sword for the dispatchers of the Austrian imperial military office, the high military veterinary school, technical clerks of the military committee, military documentary evidence clerks and military instructors and fencers from the year 1911. The hilt is of brass, the blade is 74—79 cm long and 2.9 cm wide. Adjustierungsvorschrift für das k. u. k. Heer, Wien, 1911, VII, p. 18.

199 A sword for Austrian statistics officials, accountants and building statistics officials from the year 1878. The blade is straight, 74 to 79 cm long and 2.6 cm wide. A serpent and oak leaves form the hilt's narrow guard which runs upwards out of the cross-guard, the upper end being inserted in the pommel, which is in the shape of a lion's head. On the outer side of the cross-guard there is a shell which is bent downwards and bears the Austrian eagle on it. The grip is of mother-of-pearl. Adjustierungs- u. Ausrüstungs Vorschrift für das k. u k. Heer, Wien 1878, p. 418.

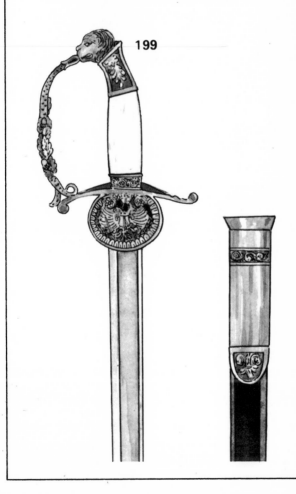

199

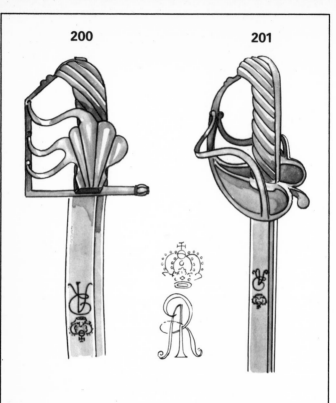

200   A Saxon infantry sword from the 18th century. The slightly curved blade is 58.7 cm long and 2.9 cm wide. On either side it bears the monogram AR and a coronet. The hilt is of brass. On the outer side the ridged guard plate bends upwards; from it run three counter-guards which connect with the knuckle bow. This type of weapon was also used in the Baden army around the year 1780. Gerd Maier: Süddeutsche Blankwaffen, Oberhöfen w. d., II. Owner: MM.

201   A Saxon sword from the 18th century. The blade is 72 cm long, 2.9 cm wide and bears the monogram AR and a coronet. The hilt is of brass. The plate is heart-shaped. The knuckle bow is connected with the sides of the shell by a counter-guard on each side. On the inner side there is a thumb ring. T.l. 86 cm, wt. 1.01 kg. Owner: MM.

202 A so-called broadsword of the Prussian artillery from the second
half of the 18th century. The blade is straight, two-edged. The
hilt is made of brass and consists of a knuckle bow and an outer
counter-guard. T.l. 71.5 cm, wt. 0.56 kg. Owner: MM.

202

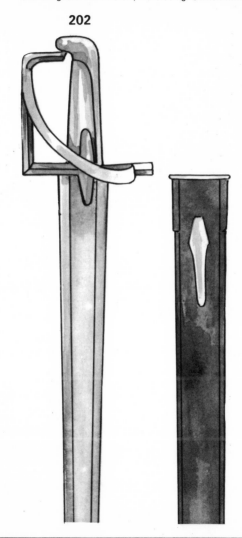

203 A Prussian grenadier sabre from the time of King Frederick William
I. The blade is slightly curved, 59 cm long, 3.1 cm wide. On the
outer side it bears the monogram FWR and a coronet and beneath
it the word: POTZDAM. On the inner side a flaming hand grenade
is engraved. The hilt is of brass. T.l. 72 cm, wt. 0.95 kg. Owner:
MM.

203

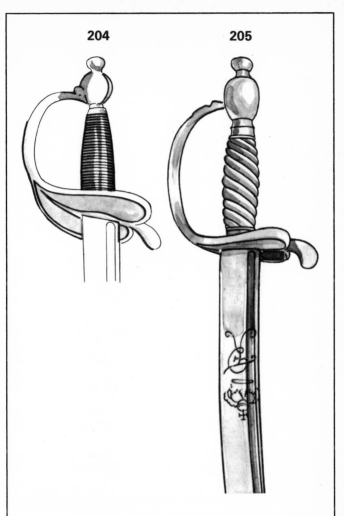

204 An English infantry hanger from 1742. Ffoulkes, p. 43, fig. 36 (A).

205 A Prussian infantry sabre from the time of King Frederick II. The blade is slightly curved, 58.7 cm long and 2.9 cm wide. It has a long narrow groove on each side and bears the monogram FR and a coronet. The hilt is of brass, with a heart-shaped plate. T.l. 74 cm. Owner: MM.

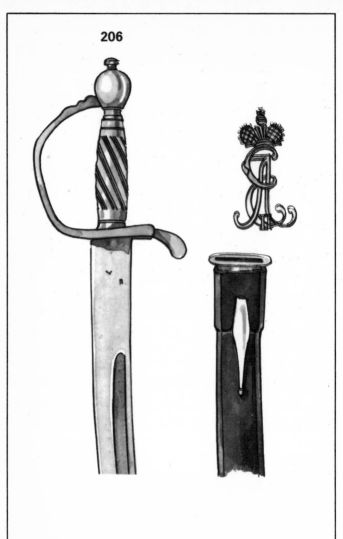

206

206   A Russian grenadier sabre from 1783. The blade is slightly curved, 66 cm long and 3.2 cm wide. On the outer side it bears the monogram of Tsarina Catherine II, EA II (Ekaterina Alekseyevna). The hilt is of brass and from a heart-shaped shell there projects a narrow knuckle guard. T.l. 81.5 cm, wt. 0.94 kg. Owner: MM.

207 A 'prima plana' Hungarian infantry sabre from the years 1740 to 1748 (Austria). Already in the Landsknecht regiments the 'prima plana' were the members of the aristocratic or landed nobility who, when enlisted, were registered on the first page. Later they came to include all those who did not stand lined up in the ranks, namely officers, subalterns and musicians. The weapon bears the inscription: VIVAT MARIA THERESIA REGINA HUNGARIAE ET BOHEMIAE and the Hungarian and Bohemian national emblems, the latter being rather unclear. The back rib of the grip ends in a lion's head. Owner: MM.

207

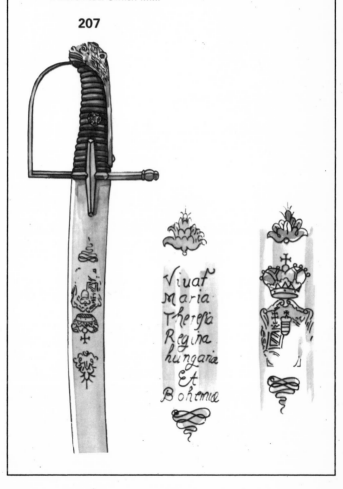

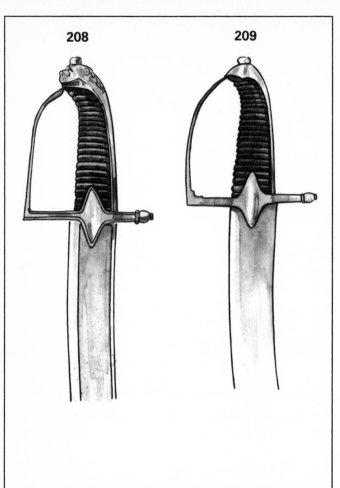

208   A sabre of a senior non-commissioned officer of the Austrian 'prima plana' infantry, from the years 1767—1777. The blade is slightly curved, 69 cm long and 3.8 cm wide. The brass hilt is narrow and the back rib ends in a lion's head. T.l. 82.5 cm, wt. 0.78 kg. Owner: MM.

209   An Austrian grenadier's sabre from 1765. The blade is slightly curved, 58.5 cm long and 4 cm wide. The brass hilt is narrow, with a smooth back rib. T.l. 71.5 cm, wt. 0.70 kg. The scabbard is of leather, with brass mounts. Owner: MM.

210 A Bavarian infantry sabre from 1794. The length of the slightly curved blade is 57 cm, the width 3.2 cm. On the outer side is the monogram CT (Carl Theodor, 1724—1799) with a coronet and beneath it a simple ornament. The same ornamentation can be found on the other side, but in addition there is the date 1794. The guard consists of a simple brass knuckle bow. The grip is covered with leather. T.l. 70 cm, wt. 0.50 kg. Owner: MM.

211 A French grenadier's sabre, M. 1790. The blade is slightly curved, 58 cm long, 3.5 cm wide. On the outer side there is a monogram consisting of two Ls placed back to back (Louis XVI, 1754—1793), on the inner the word: GRENADIER. On the back edge is engraved: M^{ture} R-le D'alsace. The hilt is made of brass. T.l. 72.3 cm, wt. 0.97 kg. Owner: MM.

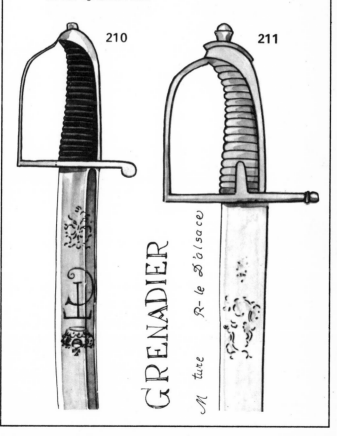

212

212   A Saxon infantry sabre from the second half of the 18th century.
The blade is straight, 59 cm long, 2.8 cm wide. The monogram
FA (Friedrich Augustus, 1750—1827) and a coronet are engraved
on both sides. The hilt is of brass, with a plain and slender knuckle
bow. T.l. 72 cm, wt. 0.62 kg. Owner: MM.

213 The French infantry sabre, *sabre briquet*, M. AN IX from 1812. The blade is slightly curved, 59 cm long and 3.5 cm wide. On the back edge is engraved: M^{fture} Imp^{le} de Klingenthal août 1812. The hilt is of brass. T.l. 73 cm, wt. 0.97 kg. Owner: MM.

213

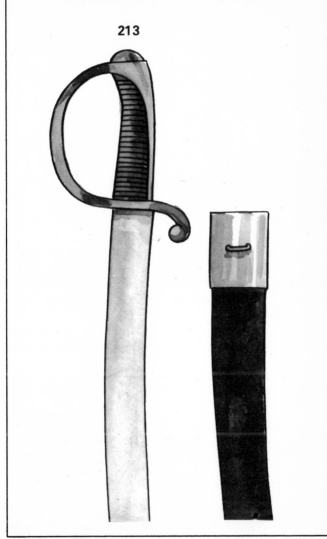

214 A Prussian infantry sabre, M. 1818 O/St, known as the 'new Prussian sabre'. It has a brass hilt. This weapon was modelled on the lines of the French infantry *sabre briquet,* M. AN IX. It was adopted largely on account of the large numbers of weapons of this type that were plundered in 1813. AWU vol. I, pp. 13—14, fig. 5. Owner: MM.

214

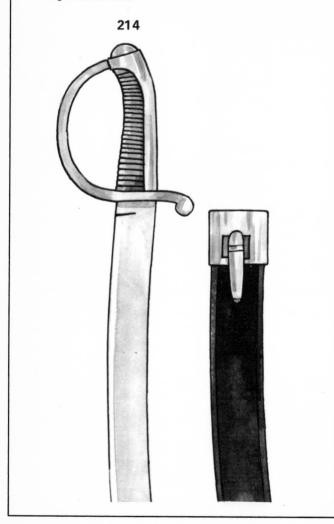

215 A Russian infantry sword from the first half of the 19th century. It was introduced into the Russian Army, and the Prussian army, after Napoleon I's defeats in the years 1812—1815 when the French infantry swords were taken as booty by the victors. This particular sword was, however, made in Russia. On the outer side of the blade there is the Russian imperial emblem and on the inner side the ruler's monogram, both of which are rather indistinct. Owner: MM.

215

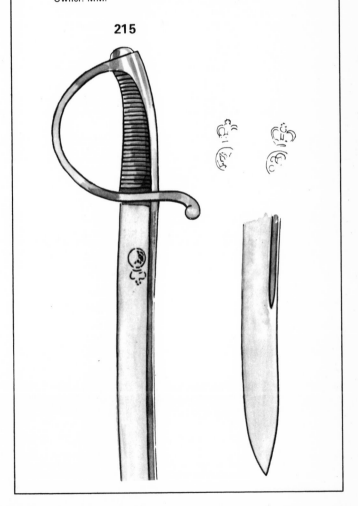

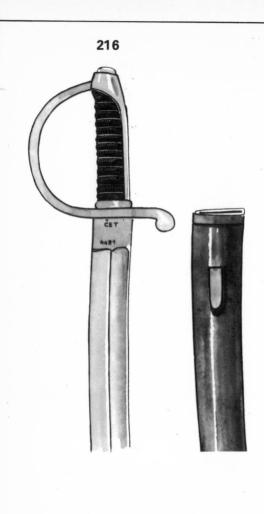

216

216 The service sabre of the Czechoslovak gendarmes. The short blade is slightly curved and the hilt consists of a simple knuckle bow of white metal. The scabbard is of iron. Owner: MM.

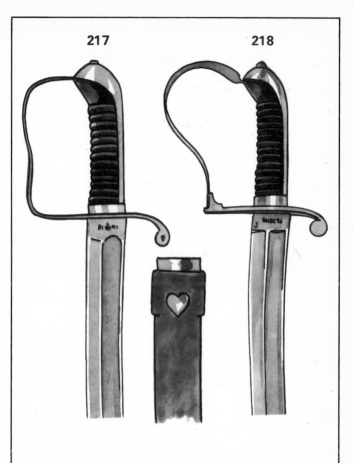

217 An Austrian infantry sabre, M. 1836. The blade is slightly curved, grooved on both sides, 65 cm long and 3.2 cm wide. The hilt is slender, with the upper part of the knuckle bow widening out. T.l. 78 cm, wt. 0.55 kg. The scabbard is of leather, with steel mounts and a heart-shaped suspension stud at the top. Owner: MM.

218 An Austrian infantry sabre, M. 1862. The slightly curved blade is grooved on both sides; l. 65 cm, w. 3.3 cm. The steel hilt is slender, with the knuckle bow slightly indented at the centre. T.l. 80 cm, wt. 0.90 kg. The scabbard is of leather, with iron mounts and a heart-shaped suspension stud. Owner: MM.

219   A sword of the Saxon janissaries from around 1700. The blade is
straight, single-edged, with the point on the back edge; l. 65.5 cm,
w. 4.6 cm. The monogram AR and a coronet can be seen on either
side of the blade. The grip, quillons and languets are of brass and
were cast in one piece. The monogram AR is also at the centre of
the quillons. T.l. 80.5 cm, A. Diener-Schönberg: Die Waffen der
Wartburg, Berlin 1912, pp. 106—107, Pl. 57, fig. 416. Owner:
MM.

219

220

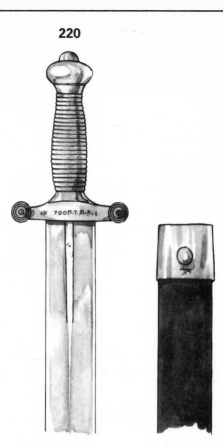

220 A Russian artillery sword from 1862. The length of the straight, two-edged blade is 48.3 cm, the width 4.2 cm. The grip is of brass, cast in one piece. The arms of the quillons terminate in whorls laid sideways and ornamented with four concentric circles. T.l. 63.5 cm, wt. 1.22 kg. The wooden scabbard is covered with leather and has brass mounts. The infantry service corps of the French artillery were equipped with a sword of this type in 1816. Both these types of weapon are roughly of the same size and weight. Owner of both these types of weapons: MM.

221 A Prussian infantry sword, M. 1852. It has a straight, one-edged blade, slightly broadening towards the point, and a back-edge point; l. 47.9 cm. The hilt is of brass. Originally this weapon was part of the equipment of the fusilier battalions of the infantry guards and the first battalion of the 1st, 2nd, 5th, 6th, 7th, 8th, 9th, 12th, 17th, 23rd, 26th and 30th regiments. AWU, vol. 1, Pl. 6. Owner: MM.

221

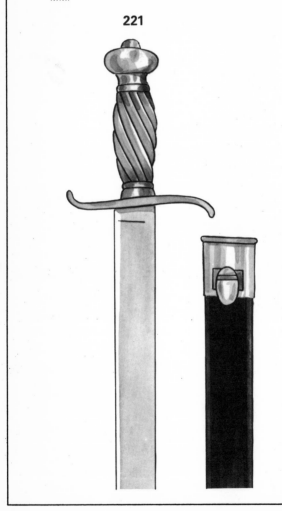

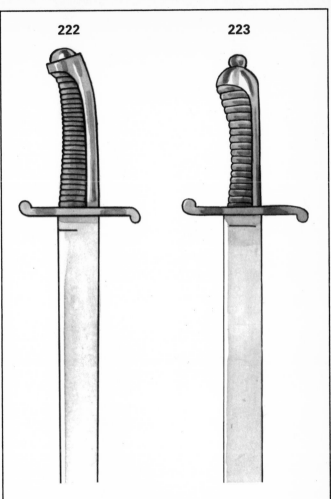

222   A Prussian infantry sword from around 1839. AWU, vol. I, pp. 13—14, Pl. 7.

223   A Saxon fusilier's sword, M. 1845. The straight single-edged blade is 47.6 cm long and 3.3 cm wide. The grip is of brass, horizontally ridged with the back rib as a decoration. The quillons are slightly S-shaped. T.l. 61.5 cm, wt. 0.85 kg. AWU, vol. I, p. 14, Pl. 3. Owner: MM.

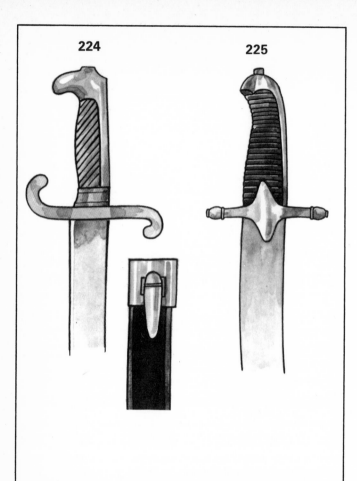

224 The Prussian general infantry sword from 1864, model U/M. The length of the slightly curved blade is 43.4 cm, the width 3.5 cm. The hilt cast in one piece is of brass, and the quillons are S-shaped. T.I. 56.3 cm, wt. 0.82 kg. AWU, Vol. I, pp. 13—15, Pl. 8. Owner: MM.

225 An Austrian fusilier's sword, M. 1765. The blade is slightly curved, 52 cm long and 3.5 cm wide. The grip is covered with leather and has a brass back rib. The quillons and langets are of brass. T.I. 65.5 cm, wt. 0.62 kg. The sabre M. 1780 is virtually the same, except that it has slightly S-shaped quillons. Owner: MM.

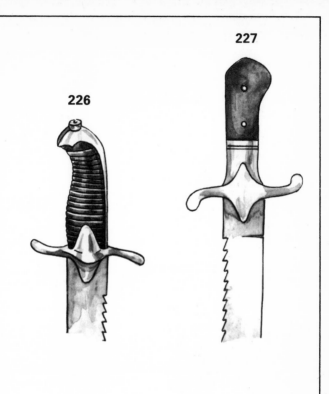

226

227

226 An Austrian sapper's sidearm, M. 1807. The blade is slightly curved, 61 cm long and 3.5 cm wide. On the back edge it has a row of double-sawed teeth. The grip has a brass back rib and quillons which are slightly S-shaped. T.l. 73.5 cm, wt. 0.90 kg. Owner: MM.

227 An Austrian sapper's sidearm from 1773. The blade is slightly curved, 55 cm long and 3.8 cm wide, and has a saw back. The lower part of the grip is of brass, as are the slightly S-shaped quillons. The upper part of the grip is bone and fixed with two rivets. T.l. 68.5 cm, wt. 0.80 kg. Owner: MM.

228 A German pioneer sidearm from the years 1810—1856. The strong
blade has a saw back edge. The hilt is of brass. It was also carried
by the stretcher-bearers. ZHW V, p. 328, Pl. 15. Owner: MM.

229 A Russian sapper's sidearm from 1827. The blade is slightly curved
and has a saw back; l. 49.2 cm, w. 5.7 cm. The hilt is of brass and
has slightly S-shaped quillons. T.l. 63.5 cm, wt. 1.22 kg. The
scabbard is wooden, covered with leather and has brass mounts.
Owner: MM.

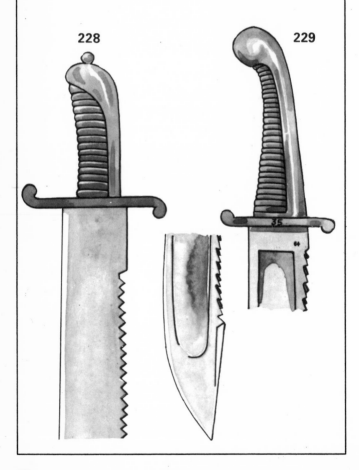

228

229

230 An Austrian sapper's sidearm from 1764. The blade is slightly curved, 63 cm long and 4 cm broad, and has a saw back. The slender hilt is made of brass. T.l. 77 cm, wt. 0.85 kg. Owner: MM.

231 An English pioneer sword from the years 1856—1903. A simple slender hilt protects the hand. The weapon has the characteristic saw back edge. Ffoulkes, p. 43, Pl. 36 (D).

230

231

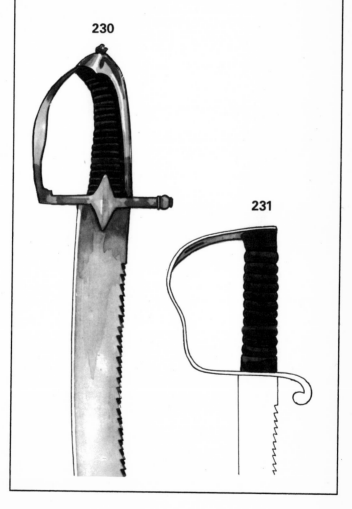

232 An Austrian pioneer sidearm, M. 1862 *(Faschinenmesser)*. The blade is straight, one-edged and grooved on the outer side; l. 46 cm, w. 5.4 cm. The grip is of bone and is secured by four rivets. The steel quillons are straight. T.l. 62.5 cm, wt. 1.15 kg. The wooden scabbard is covered with leather and has brass mounts. Owner: MM.

233 An Austrian pioneer sidearm from the First World War. The blade is straight, single-edged, 39.2 cm long and 4.1 cm wide. The grip is of wood, the steel quillons are slightly S-shaped. T.l. 54 cm. The scabbard is of steel. Owner: MM.

234　An Austrian naval sword (French type) from 1849. The blade is slightly curved, 68 cm long and 3.5 cm broad. The Austrian eagle is engraved on the outer side and has a diagonally placed anchor on the inner. On the back edge is engraved: Manuf^{re} R^{le} de Châtellerault Août 1841. The grip is covered with a metal plate. The massive hilt is made of steel and on the outer side there is an iron plate to protect the hand. The hilt is lacquered black. T.l. 82 cm. The scabbard is wooden, covered with black leather. Owner: MM. The French model is from 1833. It is of the same size and the anchor on the inner side is placed along the axis of the blade.

234

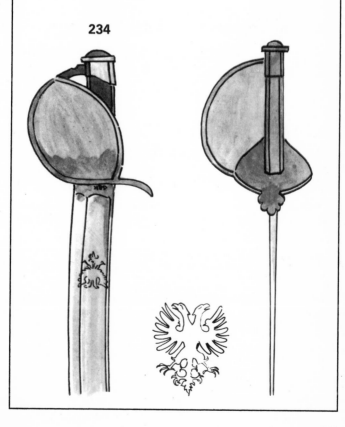

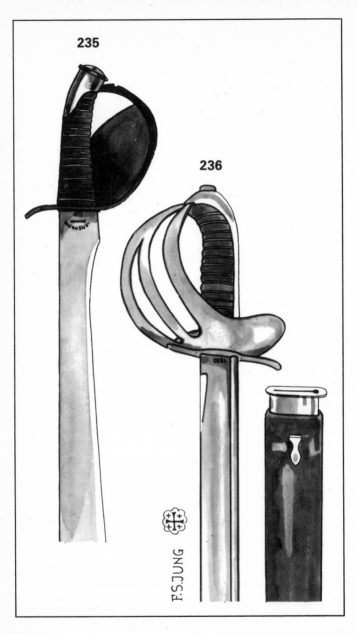

235

236

F.S.JUNG

235 A Prussian naval sword from the years 1850—1860. The blade is straight, broadening towards the point; l. 58 cm, w. 4.2 cm. It bears the name of the maker: LEMEN & JUN SOLINGEN. The grip is covered with leather. The iron hilt is asymmetrical, and on the outer side there is a guard plate of iron, protecting the hand. T.l. 74 cm. Owner: MM.

236 The new type of sword for the Austrian navy, M. 1862. The blade is straight, with a rounded back edge developing into a rib at the point. On it is stamped the name of the firm: E. S. JUNG and a Cross of Jerusalem. The iron hilt protects the hand with a knuckle bow and two counter-guards. The scabbard is covered with leather and has metal mounts. Owner: MM.

237 A Russian naval sword from 1857. The length of the slightly curved blade is 72 cm, the width 3.5 cm. The back edge is rounded and develops into a rib towards the point. The grip ends in an steel cap and is covered with leather. The iron hilt is reinforced in the lower part, the base consisting of an asymmetrical guard plate. T.l. 86.5 cm, wt. 1.10 kg. The wooden scabbard has iron mounts. Owner: MM.

237

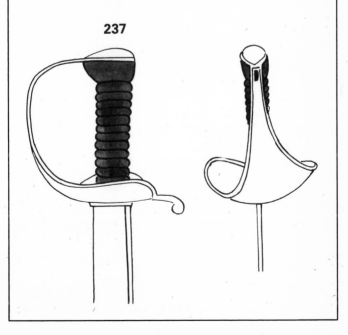

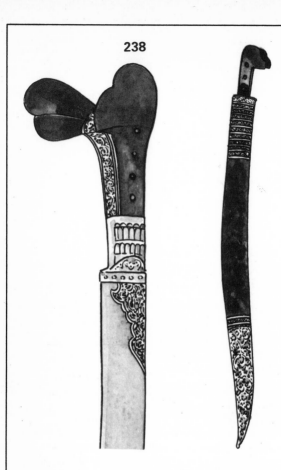

238

238   A hanger or yataghan which was part of the equipment of the members of the Serbian volunteer corps of the Austrian army in 1798. However, we come across this weapon, which is of a specific national character, as late as 1848. The blade has a double curve; l. 58.5 cm, w. 3 —3.2 cm. The grip is of horn or bone and divides at the top into two broad wings. The lower part of the grip is often ornamented with beaten silver in such a way that the ornamentation extends to the blade as well. The grip is frequently decorated with coral. The scabbard is wooden, covered with leather and massive metal mounts. Teuber —Ottenfeld, p. 831.

239 A Cherkess kindjhal. The blade of this typical Caucasian weapon is two-edged, straight, 35 cm long and narrowing to a very sharp point. On each side there is a single groove placed off centre, diagonally to one another. The grip is of horn or bone and may sometimes be of silver. The wooden scabbard is covered with leather and ornamented with silver mounts. On the upper band there is a small lug. The bottom of the chape is fitted with a knob. Owner: MM.

239

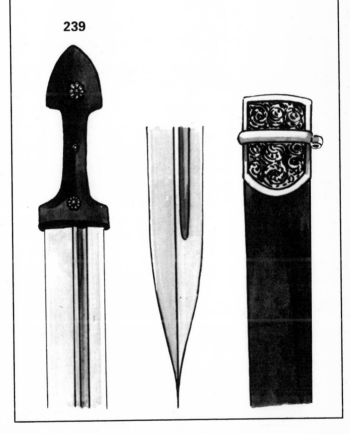

240 A Russian artillery kindjhal from 1914. The slightly curved blade is two-edged, 43.5 cm long and 3.5 cm wide. Each face has two furrows. The grip is of wood and fixed with two rivets and a brass pommel. T.l. 59 cm. The scabbard is wooden, covered with leather and lacquered and with brass mounts. Owner: MM.

240

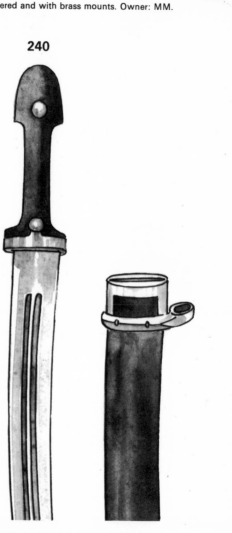

241

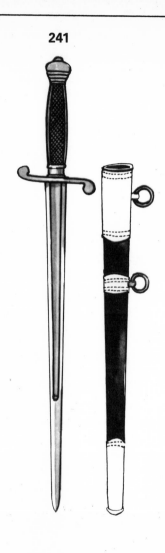

241 An Austrian naval officer's regulation dagger of 1837, worn when
on duty on board. Abbildungen zur Adjustierungs-Vorschrift für
die k. k. Armee vom Jahre 1827.

242 A dagger carried by the air crew of the Czechoslovak Air Force. The two-edged blade is 22 cm long and 2.5 cm wide. The brass hilt is fitted with a white grip. The cross-guard curves slightly upwards on both sides. At its centre is an oval design with a small Czechoslovak national emblem. T.I. 36 cm. The scabbard is of brass and is covered with two layers of brown leather: Owner: MM.

242

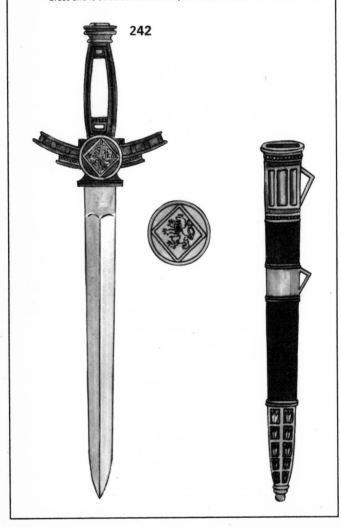

CLASSIFICATION OF THE CUT AND THRUST WEAPONS INCLUDED IN THIS BOOK